Couture Interiors

Couture Interiors

Marnie Fogg

Laurence King Publishing

Contents

Page 2. Fabrics from the interior collection by Celia Birtwell.

Radical fashion designer Vivienne Westwood with her 'Squiggle' rug, a design that first appeared in her iconoclastic 'Pirate' fashion collection in 1981.

Introduction

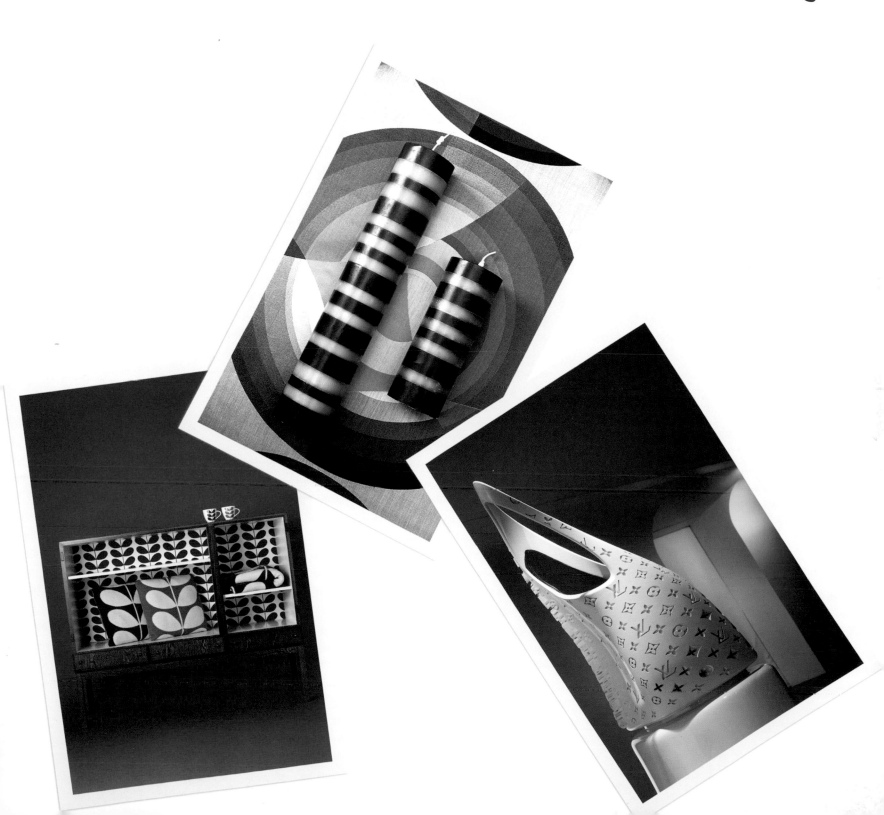

It was the Parisian couturier Christian Dior who said that 'haute couture is one of the last repositories of the marvellous'.[1] He was referring to a fashion system that represents the singular vision of a designer expressed through the medium of the best materials, a remarkable quality of make and with an unerring eye for detail. During the twenty-first century fashion designers and globally established labels are increasingly extending this aesthetic into interiors and products for the home as a natural progression from clothing the body.

The relationship between fashion and interiors is both complex and inevitable. The traditional view is that designing for interiors is somehow less subject to the whims of fashionability than for clothes, and that interior trends evolve more gradually. The difference now is in the proliferation of ideas, the speed of manufacture and the global reach of the manufacturing agencies.

Architecture, interiors and artefacts including dress have always been placed within the context of the prevailing culture. Adolf Loos, Austrian architect and critic, made the connection between architecture and clothing in his 1899 essay, 'The Principle of Cladding', describing the importance of dress as shelter,[2] and it is significant that a number of fashion designers, such as Italians Gianfranco Ferre and Romeo Gigli and Inaki Munoz of Spanish label Ailanto, began their training as architects. The increasing rapidity of new developments and technical processes in the twenty-first century affects the design and manufacture of buildings, artefacts and fashion. As architecture critic Deyan Sudjic observes, 'The new technical freedom to adopt virtually any shape for a building has made architecture closer to pattern-cutting a computer-generated skin to clothe a structure than to [designing] a traditional building.'[3] This cross-fertilization is not restricted to fashion designers extending their aesthetic into the interiors and product market. Industrial designers and architects such as Thomas Heatherwick

'Home has become fashion'

Rosita Missoni

Missoni Home collection with keynote fabrics and accessories.

The uncompromising, three-dimensional vision of architect Zaha Hadid is translated into the 'Icone', a strikingly complex seamless moulded handbag for Louis Vuitton. The monumental confidence of this piece is a coherent reflection of her style in both furniture design and architectural output, such as the Olympic ski jump at Innsbruck (opposite).

and Andrée Putman are being approached by fashion labels to contribute their spatial training and engineering skills to the design of accessories. Pritzker prize–winning architect Zaha Hadid has designed the 'Icone', a moulded white handbag for luxury goods label Louis Vuitton that reflects her preoccupation with form and function.

The way we distribute the clothes around our bodies and the artefacts around our homes is intrinsic to our sense of who we are; both are intensely personal expressions of how we desire to appear to the world. The desire for the right dress and the perfect sofa are both pursuits that thrill with the excitement of the chase, a search for something that both confirms and validates not only our existence but also our potential to be different. As British designer Jasper Conran says, 'In fashion, we're often selling much more than just a well made dress. We're selling a point of view that people want to buy into. It makes sense to extend that approach to

include furniture and homewares.' Certain principles are common to both. The designed object, after all, has to fulfil certain criteria of functionality and desirability whether it is a building, a garment, a range of bedlinen, a sofa or wallpaper.

Historically there has always been some ambivalence about the role of fashion in the context of interiors. The precepts of modernism, the defining architectural style of the twentieth century, demanded that form followed function and resisted decorative display. The assumption is that fashion constitutes an undesirable novelty that undermines such values as longevity and value for money, the idea of change being fundamental to the fashionable process. There remains in the design world a precept that it is the social responsibility of the designer 'to produce only that which will improve life…and last the vagaries of time',[4] a worthy aim, but one subverted by the pure pleasure to be found in the new, the ephemeral,

the covetable. We do not only buy shoes for their practicality; on the contrary, that may be the least of their attributes. A pair of Christian Louboutin shoes with 5-inch (12 cm) heels is certainly not fit for purpose, unless that purpose is simply to provide pleasure in their gorgeousness.

Fashion only survives because of the desire for change and innovation, clothes are replaced even when they are fully functional; if consumers bought clothes simply because the old ones were worn out, fashion would not exist. Notions of timelessness and durability, once desirable concepts, are not now necessarily perceived as virtues either in fashion or interiors. Californian design company Blik Graphics creates self-adhesive transfers that transform a room in minutes, 'for people who change their mind'.[5] Even exceptional pieces of antique furniture are subject to the vagaries of fashion. Antique shops are a powerful influence on designers and decorators, and the rise and fall of saleroom prices for the

Orla Kiely's handmade open cabinet (opposite), embellished with her signature prints, is a nostalgic homage to the modernist era and post-World War II confidence. The atelier production of such contemporary pieces contrasts with the mass-produced originals of the 1950s, which were disseminated into a wider market through a newly popular mass media, such as Britain's *House and Garden* magazine (below).

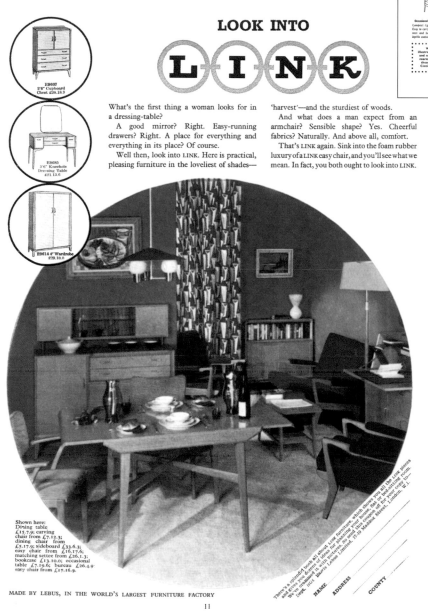

art, artefacts and furniture of previous ages are directly related to the prevailing style of the day. The current fall in value of 'brown' furniture and Victoriana, and the desirability of twentieth-century modern, encapsulates the contemporary desire to retrieve the special pieces of the 1930s, 1940s and 1950s.

Design is now being marketed and sold in much the same way that art has been, with collectors such as Bernaud Arnault of luxury goods brand LVMH (Moët Hennessy Louis Vuitton) buying as an investment for the future from gallery spaces such as Jousse Entreprise and Patrick Seguin rather than from retailers. Serious collectors concentrate on prototypes and limited editions by names such as Jean Prouve, whose work is being critically revalued to the extent that pieces such as his 'EM' table are once again in production by Swiss furniture manufacturer Vitra. The prototype for globally recognized designer and architect Zaha Hadid's 'Acqua Table' sold for a record-breaking US$298,000 in 2005, and has only increased in value.

Zeev Aram, owner of the eponymous furniture and product design store in London's Covent Garden and the retailer responsible for retrieving designer Eileen Gray from obscurity, says, 'During the 1940s Charles Eames came up with the fantastic design solution of moulded plywood to produce a single shell chair that would be comfortable without upholstery and that could be quickly mass produced. These products are actually made much better now, but people prefer to spend fantastic amounts of money on the originals because it is another way of showing the world that they are in touch with the avant-garde and have a lot of money to spend. It's not about the product.' Although iconic fashion pieces enter the auction houses, their prices generally reflect the cost of the new – a contemporary couture item will currently start at £15,000 for the simplest garment, a similar sum to that which a vintage piece of Christian Dior from the 1950s could command at auction.

In some cases the desirability of objects seems to bear little relationship to their intrinsic value, which may not necessarily reside in the integrity of the materials or the quality of make, but is to do with innovation, subversion of materials, style and surface. Decades of a design culture in thrall to modernism or minimalism has left the consumer desirous of detail, tolerant of whimsy and eager for the playful. This allows Italian fashion label Missoni to use offcuts of their bright signature fashion knits to clothe a vase and Dutch designer Maarten Baas to torch classic items of furniture and then coat the charred remains in epoxy resin. More seems to be the new less.

An increasingly visually literate consumer bombarded by design magazines, websites that offer 'a proactive online electronic magazine that keeps you up to speed and ahead of the game', a broadcast media seemingly obsessed with home and property, and an ongoing dialogue on what constitutes 'good' design, have

New York designer and art director of Japanese design firm Mogu Stephen Burks so impressed Rosita Missoni that she handed him a bag of offcuts and told him to 'go and play'. The result is a collection of patchwork vases that exemplify the Missoni aesthetic of multicoloured effervescent space-dyed stripes.

Spectacles, waistcoat and cutlery transcend their
classic form when subjected to the decorative
impulse of Italian fashion house Etro.

all resulted in interiors and products for
the home being subject to the same desire
for innovation, change and fashionability
as fashion. The media is responsible for
directing the public's gaze towards a new
trend or a 'hot' designer. As Zeev Aram
points out: 'The art director of a magazine
is enormously influential in dictating
public taste. They are the ones who decide
what is for public consumption. A lot
of young designers are built up because
they are the "next big thing", just as they
are in fashion. The magazines might
feature a particular image of something
because it fits well on the page, rather than
illustrating the capabilities of the designer.
Often reputation exceeds performance.'

The forerunner of the plethora of interior
design publications such as *Elle Decoration*
and *World of Interiors* appeared in 1897.
Founded by businessman John Benn,
The House strove to educate a consumer
challenged by choice. As the number of
these titles increased throughout the inter-

war years subsequent magazines, whilst
disseminating trends, rarely strayed into the
fashionable arena or wrote about 'lifestyle'.
The word 'lifestyle' was not yet in common
usage, but as early as 1928 Margaret Case
on the staff of American *Vogue* said, 'There
is so much more to *Vogue* than clothes. It's
fashion in living that we present. We're
the first to do these things.'[6] Editors of
contemporary publications realize that an
audience for the latest in interior design is
also very likely to be interested in fashion.
As Mark Eley of design duo Eley Kishimoto
points out, 'the media that surrounds fashion
and interiors speaks to the same audience.'

The rapid development of new
technologies and innovatory materials
sustains the content of these magazines
and has an immediate impact on the
conjunction of ideas and trends such as
laser cutting and flocking. Designer and
retailer Sir Paul Smith acknowledges this
confluence. 'I think most creative industries
run in parallel to each other and fashion

The eclectic and sumptuous surfaces and imaged fabrics of the Day Birger et Mikkelsen fashion collection have been deployed into richly decorated interiors and accessories.

and interiors are no exception. If you look at the mid 1980s fashion was very minimal; black suits, white shirts and so were the interiors. In fact this style of interior has lasted a long time, but slowly, like fashion, interiors are now more about a mix of pattern and colour. For instance, the modern interior now could have wallpaper, rugs in colour, and things found on vacation such as ceramics or other artefacts.' Marianne Brandi, designer of the Day Birger et Mikkelsen home collection, agrees: 'We all have a great desire for creating a home that expresses who we are, our personal style and what we stand for. I think that people in general are very good at achieving a contemporary look but with a twist, meaning that they have something familiar, something modern and something classic that makes their home personal to them.'

Occasionally it is the designer's involvement in creating a retail environment representative of their merchandise that becomes the first step in translating a

signature pattern from a garment on to walls and prompts a foray into the accessories end of the homeware market. More particularly, there is evidence that furniture and homeware producers have not yet fully recognized the power of marketing a brand, leaving the way open for fashion designers to capitalize on the urgent desire of the consumer to enjoy the latest trends from a high profile designer name. Sheridan Coakley, founder of leading London design store SCP and design brand Case, relates the way in which the furniture industry now operates as the fashion industry once did in the 1960s. 'The furniture industry is innovative and exciting, but it is also fragmented, amateurish and seriously underdeveloped as an industry, just as fashion was in the 1960s. There is a gap in the interiors market and fashion designers have been quick to see this. Fashion has internationally strong brands, business models that go from the high end of the market, such as

The 'high quality, high volume' home collection is produced for London retailers Sheridan Coakley and Paul Newman to the specifications of established designers. Top, 'Hoot' cabinet by Terence Woodgate; above, 'Loop' bed by Nazanin Kamali; and opposite, extending table by Matthew Hilton.

Gucci, to the lower end with Gap and Zara. In Europe there is no middle ground in furniture; it is either cheap or overpriced.'

Together with designer Paul Newman, Coakley is addressing this lack with Case, a collection of high-quality furniture designed by such names as Matthew Hilton and Robin Day, but produced in greater quantities, and thus more cheaply. 'The Americans have resolved this middle ground problem with a company called Design Within Reach. It was originally Web-based, but they now have 70 stores and their motto is "in store and ready to ship", rather than the 12 weeks' wait there would be for items in Europe. They have adopted fashion working practices; better marketing, quicker turn around and manufacturing at higher volume to lower the prices. Fashion has a very sophisticated understanding of marketing and creating products'. He makes the point. 'Ask people to name five furniture designers, and the odds are that they wouldn't be able to. Ask the same people to nominate five fashion designers, and their names would probably come easily to mind.'

Tunisian born designer Tom Dixon, responsible as creative director for the successful revival of British company Habitat, is also using the paradigm of fashion labels such as Louis Vuitton and Burberry to bring together his diverse activities into a recognizable brand. His practice, which now includes expanding his own fashion-led label and working with Finnish furniture company Artek also encompasses architecture, clothing and cars. 'The model of being a travelling designer, working for different companies, makes it difficult to get mass recognition of what your aesthetic is,' he states. 'I'm trying to replicate something closer to what happens in fashion by having my own label.'[7] To this end a chain-link logo appears on fabrics, laminates, wallpapers, carpets and furniture. This move away from the anonymity of the studio to a personality-driven brand is entirely in

Number 9 Albemarle Street is British fashion designer Paul Smith's response to the homogenization of the shopping experience. This unique collection of unusual objects, furniture and pieces is located in the heart of London's Mayfair.

keeping with the desire of the designers to market themselves as individuals, and very much a reflection of the influence of the fashion industry on that of interiors.

Unlike fashion, which apart from brief excursions into various dress reform movements has never been of sociological intent, product design has always historically been connected to some sort of utopian ideal whereby good design is industrially manufactured in great numbers to serve the requirements of the masses. This would be a difficult case to defend now. Increasingly, avant-garde pieces are the prerequisite of an elite group of designers such as Patricia Urquiola and Marcel Wanders, all working for the same group of manufacturers. In fashion this desire for the special piece is accommodated by the burgeoning phenomenon of demi-couture, a product pitched between industrially produced designer fashion, ready-to-wear and the entirely handmade

haute couture specifically fitted on the client and with an unknown price tag.

Fashion companies have been quick to seize the opportunity of the economic potential of extending their brands into the home sector. Growth is a prerequisite for all companies, and for businesses to grow there are two ways forward: selling more of the product to existing customers or selling the same product to new customers. Venturing into the homeware market allows businesses to do both, but with the advantage that the brand already has credibility and cachet. As Paul Smith says, 'A lot of designers have home collections, but I don't think this is about interiors. Often they are part of big groups who are under pressure to expand and get more sales; homewares are one of the ways to do this.'

The branding of products has existed since the age of mass manufacture in the nineteenth century, a system that replaced anonymous commodities with something universally recognized, usually by its logo

or packaging. According to style commentator Peter York, CEO of brand strategy consultancy SRU, the nature of branding changed in the 1980s. He asks, 'What put this rather socially suspect brandology mind-set absolutely centre stage in modern commerce and culture? Globalisation for a start, which uprooted every settled relationship going, and there was new technology, new product sectors for a more prosperous and sophisticated world...and, latterly "luxury goods".'[8] As the decade progressed branding emerged as a tangible asset alongside the more conventional ones of factory space and stock and equally deserving of financial valuation. In contemporary terms, it is vital to a company's success, particularly in the luxury goods market when licensing has to be an option. The value of the brand name can be seen in the way its reputation is rigorously observed and protected. Brands can easily be debased by an inappropriate connection with the customer from hell, particularly in the fashion arena. Celebrities are not always the most appropriate showcases for a luxury goods label, and may be one of the reasons why there is usually a backlash against such conspicuous consumption, as happened after the excesses of the 1980s. Luxury may no longer mean the affirmation of wearing or using the right brand, but may involve a search for the exclusive, elusive product that is evidence of the consumer's discernment and refined sensitivity.

Manufacturers of products for the home may not have the management methods to fast track ideas – something at which the fashion industry is adept. Those contemporary fashion designers who extend their range beyond the home decoration market – ceramics, cushions and glassware – into furniture usually do so in conjunction with a furniture manufacturer, as is the case with Paul Smith and his collection for Cappellini, and the collaboration between Issey Miyake and Ron Arad. In contrast, some designers are content to simply license their fabrics to the manufacturers.

High-profile fashion designers such as Ralph Lauren and Donna Karan have long understood the importance of global branding and the marketing of a total look that is rooted in a visible and established identity, and where fashion and interiors are fused into a signature style or design ethos. Designers such as Giorgio Armani understand that their customers require interiors that reflect a similar aesthetic to their fashion labels. Consumers do not just want to buy clothes; they want to buy into a lifestyle and a provenance.

The symbiosis between ideas for fashion and ideas for interiors has never been more robust, whether it concerns sources of inspiration, trends in materials or innovative practices. As Rosita Missoni, co-founder of the eponymous Italian fashion company replied when asked why a number of fashion designers were expanding into interior ranges, 'because I think home has become fashion.'

Devoid of clothes, the interior of the Paul Smith shop displays 'really quirky one-off things that I have picked up from my travels and fallen in love with. It's a curiosity shop, a place where you might find a piece of museum-quality furniture or something funny and kitsch.'

Chapter one *Inspiration*

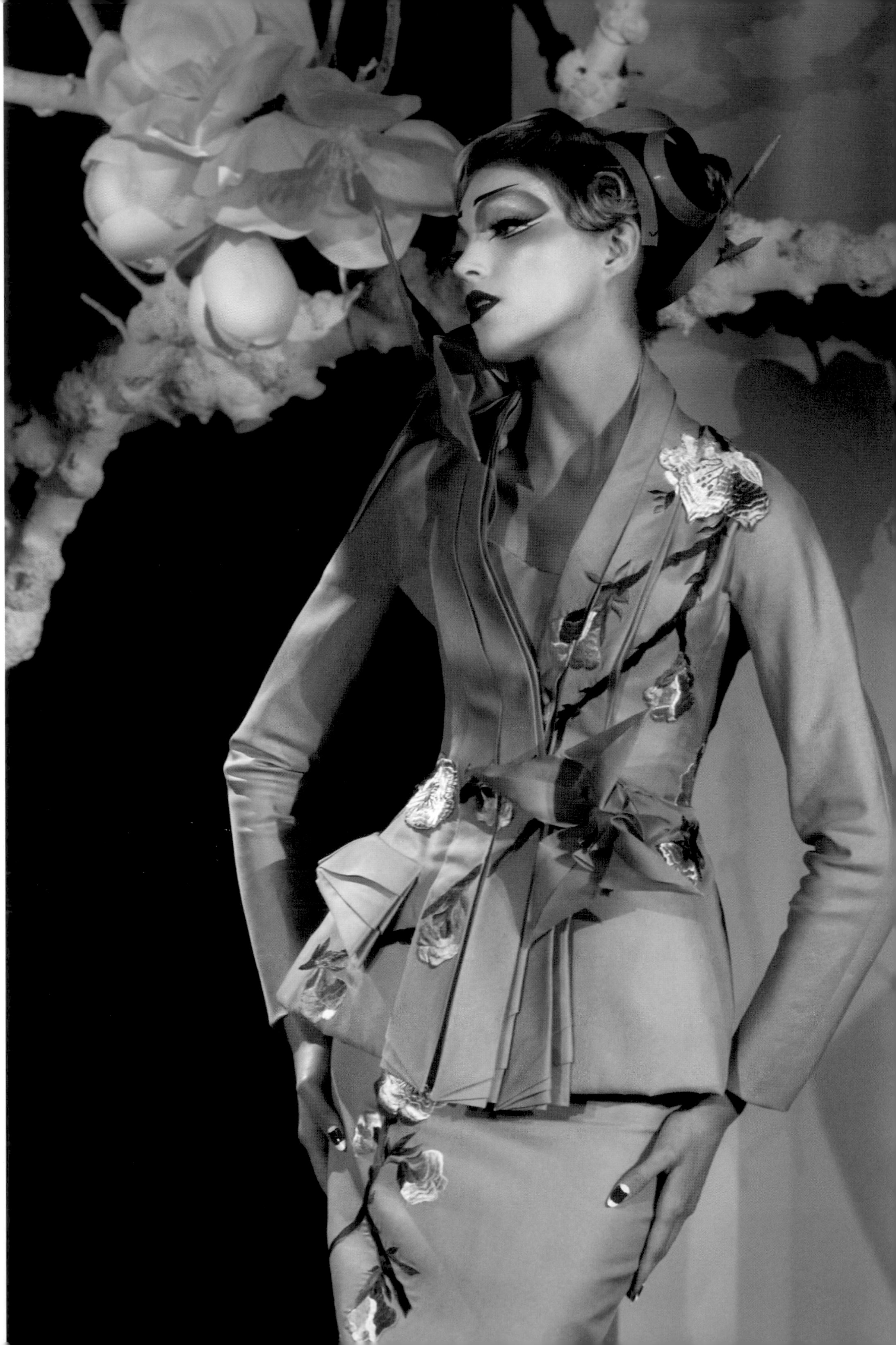

Couture on the catwalk presents an extreme view that cannot be replicated by large-scale manufacturers; it operates as a 'think tank' in promulgating ideas that inevitably infiltrate every aspect of design at all levels of the market. The spectacle of the fashion show is the driving force behind change, providing influential trends and raising the benchmark of creativity, respecting the authenticity of ideas and processing them with integrity. Couture clothes are the most expensive that money can buy and, if the garment is not handmade in Paris, then it cannot be called haute couture. John Galliano, creative director of the house of Dior, describes the fashion industry as a pyramid. At the uppermost point is the parfum, the purest and most potent scent, halfway down is the eau de parfum, somewhat diluted, and at the base, the eau du toilette, the most diffuse scent of the three.[1] Couture is the parfum, ready-to-wear is the eau de parfum, and the mass market, the eau du toilette. Couture interiors also reflect this hierarchy, from the bespoke furniture designers and makers at the top of the pyramid, to the mass production manufacturers such as the Spanish company Zara Home.

At every level of the market, one of the most mysterious and esoteric skills of the designer is that of knowing exactly the right time to introduce, change or enhance an idea, whether it is for a garment, homeware or a retailing concept. Couturiers and fashion designers invariably include in their budget funds for a team of assistants to explore other cultures and countries. These excursions provide an opportunity to investigate and explore not only the geographical differences, but also the narratives of the country, in which the ephemera-detritus on the streets, from bus tickets to cinema programmes, assume as much importance as the treasures in the local museum. Parisian couturiers John Galliano and Jean Paul Gaultier are

'I've long believed that the eye runs naturally from the catwalk to the kitchen.'
Anna Wintour[2]

Ranging from subtle distillation to representative evocation, John Galliano for French couture house Dior epitomizes the power of cultural research in constantly refreshing the collection. The orientalist essence in this tailored composition suggests the kimono in the simple pleated collar and the origami-like tied belt.

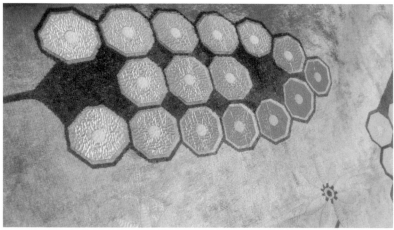

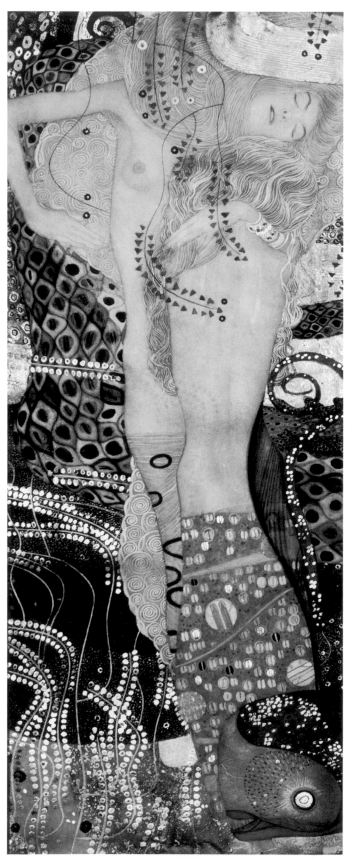

The trend for metallic surfaces has influenced all aspects of the design world, from accessories and fashion, as shown in Christopher Bailey's short metallic dress for Burberry and Ralph Lauren's gold bag, to products for the home. The glittering and textured hues of Gustav Klimt's painting, *Water Serpents I*, are reflected in the rectilinear gilded motifs of Neisha Crosland's 'Hollywood Grape' fabric and her 'Vanilla Gold Zebra' wallpaper.

both renowned for mediating these global influences through their collections, while for British designer Vivienne Westwood it is the European salons of the eighteenth century and the work of French rococo painter François Boucher that continually provide a source of inspiration.

Designers are constantly asked, 'From where do you get your ideas?' Paul Smith will reply, 'You can find inspiration in anything', but there does seem to be a collective unconscious at work, explained by that overworked word, 'zeitgeist', in which designers tap into a particular aspect of cultural activity that results in the emergence of a broad-based trend. It can seem that designers for both fashion and interiors are very often actually looking in the same place at the same time. A blockbuster exhibition such as the one held at the Los Angeles County Museum of Art in 2005 of the work of Gustav Klimt can kick-start a trend that permeates all aspects of the design world.

The exhibition showed a group of five of Klimt's early twentieth-century paintings, including a rare example of one of his famous gold paintings, of which there are only three. The five paintings are remarkable examples of Viennese high modernism, and consist of three richly textured landscapes and two portraits of Adele Bloch-Bauer, one of them the dazzling and sumptuously patterned gold painting, which dates from 1907. A highly textured and glittering surface then became the preferred medium for a multiplicity of products. Christopher Bailey's short metallic dress for Burberry was the item of the following season, and shimmery shifts by Marc Jacobs and Gucci also appeared. Louis Vuitton, Fendi and Carlos Falchi all produced a range of metallic bags, and even the traditionalist Ralph Lauren bought into the trend with his gilded leather 'Ricky' bag. Donna Karan named her scent 'Gold', and in interiors the trend was evidenced by wallpapers such as 'Million Gold' by Maya Romanoff.

Left. An inspirational sketch by Spanish designer Jaime Hayon for Camper shoes.

Opposite. The mood board shows the ideas behind a collection for Danish fashion label Day Birger et Mikkelsen. Designers very often find such devices useful: a collection of images and ephemera from which they derive inspiration and which leads the collection along a cohesive path. The narrative includes texture, colour, pattern and surface decoration.

The provenance of most trends lies in the prevailing culture of the day; even the perennial appeal of the floral pattern is mediated through diverse cultural influences; from exhibitions of the large-scale impressionistic flowers of Monet to the work of artist Frida Kahlo, which prompted a plethora of brightly coloured stylized florals on a black background. The desire for the sumptuousness of highly patterned floral silk brocades resonates with a preoccupation with the court of King Louis XVI and the palace of Versailles; Roberto Cavalli, Dolce & Gabbana and Miu Miu have all taken inspiration from 1774, and the year Marie Antoinette took the throne.

Primary research is the most vital element of the creative process, without which there is merely pastiche and replication. Such research animates, inspires and directs all aspects of design development by the designer and the design team, in which decisions are made as to yarns, fabric, texture, colour palettes, surface detail, decoration, form and silhouette. For the product designer, this research will necessarily involve an analysis of the data. Spanish designer of the Camper shoe shops, Marti Guixe, has a pragmatic approach: 'I don't believe in inspiration. I work by acquiring, having and processing information, and taking logical, coherent, reasonable decisions depending on the project in relation to its context.'[3] Other designers are less analytical; ideas might be sparked by anything and everything, from a fragment of cloth, a torn poster, the illustrations of a nineteenth-century biologist or an exhibition, to the films of Fritz Lang. Creativity is sometimes inspired by technical

Opposite. International specialist press informs fashion and interior designers about all aspects of the industry, including trend analysis, changing customer demographics, new technology in manufacturing processes and information on trade fairs and exhibitions.

Above. Arcane images, such as these from Nelly Rodi for the Pilote trend book for FW 08/09, may be seemingly divorced from their subject matter, yet they still aspire to evoke and convey the whole of a mood or trend. Their intention is that the theme of 'Utopia', defined in the image of silver bangles, should reference the 1968 film space–sex romp *Barbarella* and iconic female warrior Batwoman, whilst 'Island', an image of a chair on the beach, signifies the trend towards natural living.

developments, or is concept-led, where science takes the place of narrative. These eclectic musings are the starting point for a new collection, from which ideas for fabric, one of the first links in the production chain for both fashion and interiors, are developed.

Very few designers actually 'buy in' their cloth from trade fairs such as Premier Vision, a commercial marketing organization dedicated to promoting the textile industry, which hosts up to 800 fashion fabric manufacturers from around the world displaying and selling their work. Ready-to-wear designer/makers such as Eley Kishimoto source, dye and design their own cloth for their catwalk collections or for interior use. The majority of fashion labels include a textile designer in their studio. British designer Matthew Williamson, for instance, liaises with his textile specialist Ann Ceprynski to discuss the concept that will provide the impetus for his collections, and then works with Belford Prints on the technical developments of

the print. Those designers who do buy in fabrics from the fabric shows remain secretive about their purchases, preferring the consumer to think that all the design work on the label is done 'in house', as this protects the authenticity of the brand.

For those companies that are not led by the strong aesthetic and singular eye of a designer there are the fashion forecasters who disseminate trends that are to a certain extent already determined. Their role is to market them to the retailer and the manufacturer. It is a reversal of the 'trickle down' effect from haute couture, as youthful 'trendtrackers' or 'cool hunters' report back to style bureaux such as Nelly Rodi, pioneer of trend counselling in Europe. Their findings on street tribes and youth movements are then logged in trend books that act as inspirational tools to the mass production design industry. Pierre-François Le Louet, chief executive officer of Nelly Rodi, which has a client list that includes Agnès B., H&M, Givenchy and LVMH

Must Have Designers

Fredrikson Stallard

1855 July 10
(Edw.ᵈ Price)

CANDLE #1

BRUSH

TABLE #5

VILLOSUS

The disciplines of craft-based ceramics and product design form an unlikely but successful alliance with Fredrikson Stallard. The two designers – Patrik Fredrikson and Ian Stallard – refer to the work they create together as 'fairy tales for grown-ups'.

Their designs mix sensitivity and fragility with robust functionality. With the award-winning Rug #1, they use black urethane to create the illusion of an oil slick. Not something you'd want on your floor – or is it? Rug#2 achieves a ghoulish beauty by using two 4.8-litre volumes of red urethane to represent pools of blood from two people. Table #1 and Table #2 are raw chunks of untreated birch tied into a bunch. With the surface gaps, uneven texture and honest construction, the designers have stripped a table down to its bare essentials. Contrast this with the delicacy of Cable and Dragon – fine porcelain vessels, upright and narrow, but fortified by the addition of dragon heads or cables and leads wrapped around the body. Currently working on a new collection for David Gill, they were winners of the Arts Foundation 2006 furniture design award.

COMME DES GARÇONS, COLOGNE

Yet another of their guerrilla stores, again in a former butchers. *www.guerilla-store.com*

INSTITUTIONALISED

As the world runs out of warehouses to convert, prisons and old institutions have become the hot ticket. Watch out for a rash of interiors using abattoir tiling (handy for the full wash-down experience), asylum doors and windows, and prison fixtures and fittings. This sombre aesthetic, featuring butcher's blocks, white tiling, meat hooks, and old sanitary fittings (basins, urinals, wash areas) is already proving a hit with Comme des Garçons, who are opening up in the former butchers to the Lloyd Hotel, Amsterdam, which was also previously a prison during WWII.

LLOYD HOTEL, AMSTERDAM

This now über-stylish hotel now has a unique 1-to-5-star room choice, and runs by the motto 'luxury is our standard, economy is an option'. *www.lloydhotel.com*

JAIL HOTEL, LÖWENGRABEN, SWITZERLAND

The first Jailhotel in Switzerland, built in 1862, was used as a prison until autumn 1998. Where prisoners once attempted to escape, today's tourists and residents of Lucerne enjoy the unique atmosphere of the hotel and its Alcatraz bar. Prison memorabilia lines the corridors and each of the rooms has the original heavy wooden cell doors, complete with slots for food. *www.jailhotel.ch*

LLOYD HOTEL

MALMAISON

Previous spread. The Future Laboratory is a trends, brands and consumer insight network specializing in brand strategy and design innovation. The role of such businesses seems to be of increasing importance in an industry eager to quantify, anticipate and sustain market needs.

Above and opposite. The largest international trade fair for home and contract fabrics, Heimtextil Frankfurt, also offers the consumer the latest predictions from colour and trend specialists.

(Moët Hennessy Louis Vuitton), explains, 'If you give the same intelligence to those who sell the clothes, those who design them, those who buy the fabrics and those who supply them, there are enormous economic advantages for the fabric manufacturers because they know what material will be in demand. Similarly, if the retailers are all stocking violet that season, it inevitably creates a demand for violet, so they sell out of their stock.'[4] Le Louet adds, 'The luxury brands don't buy them often because they see themselves as trendsetters. Retailers and the beauty industry are the biggest buyers.'

The highly respected colour and trend consultant Li Edelkoort, member of KM Associates, and the founder of Trend Union, offers trend and lifestyle presentations all over the world. She founded her studio in 1991 in response to the increased demand of companies for guidance on product development, brand identity and strategies in engaging with contemporary culture to further their sales in targeting a specific

customer. She describes her role thus: 'I'm not a designer, I'm not a couturier, I'm not an illustrator; I am a forecaster. Therefore I always know what fashion has to be, or what style should be, or what lifestyle will be.'[5] These are impressive credentials, particularly the ability to predict something as inherently unpredictable as future lifestyles. Alfred Adler first used the term 'lifestyle' in 1929 to describe a person's basic character as established in early childhood that governs their reactions and behaviour. Subsequently used by Alvin Toffler in 1939 to describe a set of behaviours in making a conscious choice when matching a consumer with products, it has now been appropriated by brands as an all-encompassing way of describing their homeware ranges. It has become much more than a way of simply describing how we live, and has come to denote the aspirational nature of the merchandise, be it a range of bedlinen, a sofa or a dress.

The known demographics of the potential customer encompass everything,

'I always know what fashion has to be, or what style should be, or what lifestyle will be.'

Li Edelkoort

from location, income and class to holiday venues and food shopping. Nothing is left to chance, but marketing strategies cannot be foolproof in forecasting the future, otherwise there would be no discount stores, nor unsold clothes and products.

An online service, the Worth Global Style Network (WGSN), created in 1998 by brothers Julian and Marc Worth, is able to update its trends information on a daily basis, a facility accessed by the mass market of both fashion and interiors. The trends for interiors traditionally have had a significantly less frantic turnaround than for fashion, but increasingly there is now the same desire for information on directions, trends and colours. Fabrics and products for the home are shown at the main trade fairs, Decorex International and 100% Design, a showcase of established and emerging international brands, in September, both of global importance. Maison & Objet Editeurs, the international annual meeting of decorative fabric houses

such as Creation Baumann, Christian Fischbacher, the German firm Johannes Wellman, Luigi Bevilacqua de Venise and Pierre Frey, together with Maison & Objet and Planete Meuble Paris (Planet Furniture Paris) are an opportunity for designers to present new products to architects, decorators and hoteliers.

There is not, however, the same sense of urgency in producing a collection for interiors as there is for fashion, as these venues are not the only opportunity to sell the products. Fashion has a short timetable, namely the bi-annual catwalk shows, which is why the perception is that fashion designers are more creative, livelier and more hardworking. Wallpaper and textile designs and products for the home have a longer shelf life than fashion garments, and stay much longer in production; witness the cyclical popularity of the nineteenth-century British artist and craftsman William Morris, whose prints are still in production today.

An understanding of the importance of proportion in conveying a look of pared down elegance is evident in the modern aesthetic of British designer Jasper Conran. His understated chic extends from his catwalk collection into the products he designs for British china company Wedgwood, such as this platinum-striped tableware.

The forecasting industry has become big business, one to a certain extent that feeds on itself, one of the problems being that they are processing the same information and thus disseminating the same trends. Trendstop, a British forecasting company, offers 'global style codes, signs and signals translated into instant straight-to-market stories' with promises of certain commercial success to the subscriber. Such offers to 'factor the new street edge subculture cool into an instant application style fix to sex up your corporate package'[6] are not really aimed at the designer, but at the company that wants to be assured of its position in a marketplace where branding is all. Designers would balk at the idea that they might need a 'style fix' rather than pursue their own aesthetic in a way that is both creative and authentic. As British designer Jasper Conran points out: 'A certain segment will always follow trends because they have nothing else to guide them. Those who have developed a personal aesthetic are more immune to what's happening around them. I'm not anti-trend by any means. If it works for you – great. The problem is when a certain trend doesn't work for you but you follow it up anyway because it's popular. People need to be strong enough to say "no".' According to Tony Davis, designer and founder of design and manufacturing company Art Meets Matter, forecasting is an outdated concept. 'Companies use forecasting and try to plan ahead and produce huge quantities on the basis of that information, and then lose money because everything has to be discounted. An enormous amount of waste ensues. I think there need to be radical changes in retailing; we sell things now in the way that they sold 100 years ago. With the Internet you can get really close to the customer and ask, what is the point of this material? I don't like the idea of me being in charge and saying as a designer, "You must have this"; the future of retailing lies in it being much more interactive.'

A corner of the studio of British designer Neisha Crosland. For her, the process of creativity starts with drawing and painting in a sketchbook, which is also a place to assemble inspirational source material that is subsequently incorporated into design development on paper.

Tony Davis is not alone in having this point of view. However, the infrastructure has existed for some time now to allow for e-commerce, or mass customization, a method whereby the consumer enters into a relationship with the designer and manufacturer to customize a product, choosing colour, size, pattern or texture to fit their own personal requirements. This process has enormous potential, but seemingly only a minority of consumers wish to engage with the design process, and only a small number of manufacturers are prepared to offer this service. While scanning the Internet to pick up on the latest trends, or ordering from one of the successful shopping sites such as Net-a-Porter, the customer is engaging in shopping as a leisure activity, something to be enjoyed for its own sake rather than being proactive in the production of the product. Not every purchase is planned, and the process discounts the notion of instant gratification, as well as spontaneity. The reasons why

we enjoy shopping are complicated, and not always to do with what we buy.

The chronology and methodology of the design process is unique to each designer. For British textile and wallpaper designer Neisha Crosland it is an ongoing activity. 'You take the creative process for granted. For me, it starts with drawing, then you have to understand proportion, and finally you have to use colour like a painter.' The starting point for a collection is a sketchbook and a pinboard. 'I create a board with things that catch my eye; a piece of ribbon, postcards, photographs, creating shapes and colours. Then I snip bits off and add things; it's all very chaotic. Then I start to organize the information in the way that a biologist collects and classifies specimens. I label everything and give them working titles, which is really important. There is a moment when you become a stylist, juxtaposing things together and discarding those that don't work. Then I get a grid going, and each box contains one idea.

I spend a lot of time up a ladder so I can get a bird's-eye view – these boards are enormous – "tweaking" until I get it right.'

Crosland, whose work is archived in the Victoria & Albert Museum and the Geffrye Museum in London, produces relatively small collections, namely six wallpaper and fabric designs both in seven colourways, which are enormously influential. Crosland ascribes the current high turnover in trends in interiors to the increasing ability of manufacturers to replicate the high end of the market quickly. 'Just as in fashion the mass market can almost instantly copy what is seen on the catwalk, so it is with interior trends. Everything in the shops is the same; they are moving ideas on, but doing the same thing at the time.' This can have serious implications for the designer. 'Companies don't care enough about where the ideas come from; people don't respect the provenance of ideas enough. We encourage fair trade for products; what about fair trade for ideas?' In an ideas-led industry, provenance is all important. Crosland now registers all her designs, an expensive and time-consuming process, but one that is necessary to protect the integrity of her label. 'It is an interesting process, because you can't just copyright the whole design, someone might use just an element of it. You have to analyse what is important in the piece, and register each component, the leaf, the bud, the flower, the background stripe etc.'

For designers to develop fabrics for both fashion and interiors there has to be real understanding of how cloth performs when it is wrapped around a body or sofa, and what happens to pattern when it is placed on a 3D object. Crosland explains, 'With flat surfaces you contemplate the pattern in relation to the size of the room and the furniture.' The designer believes that pattern will always have an appeal. 'I delight in the repeat, people like pattern. There is something about the repeat that people find calming, there is a reassurance;

'If you are never stopping, you are always going.'

Neisha Crosland

The next stage for Crosland is to gather ephemera, swatches, art work, photographs and notes on a giant pinboard, which leads to the realization of the final product. The versatility of good design is evident in the use of her zebra print for a bag by international luxury leather brand Bill Amberg.

Embroidery, the art of embellishing cloth by hand or machine, has always been perceived as luxurious, supplying richness of detail with consummate craftsmanship. Although decoration is inevitably subject to design trends, embroidery continues to exert fascination with couturiers of both fashion and interiors, both of whom collaborate with embroidery and mixed-media textile designer Karen Nicol.

coming back, disappearing, coming back, disappearing.' Even in periods of modernity the pattern continues to engage the attention. 'I strip the pattern down to its bare essentials. Form follows function in that the creative process is one of distillation and filtering. The pattern has to fit on the roller, the inks cannot fade and the cloth must sustain wear. Decoration for me is about expression. It needs to work within the constraints, restrictions and possibilities of the technique that is to put the decoration on the product.'

Decoration is what gives the product a form of expression and feeling. Intelligent decoration is design, in that if it is to work it needs to be conceived and planned to suit and give character and expression to the product it is decorating. Even the decision to not decorate is a form of decoration. For Karen Nicol, an embroidery and mixed-media textile designer who works in fashion and interiors, as well as being a Research Fellow at London's Royal College of Art,

inspiration may come from many sources. Her London-based design and production studio has been established for more than 20 years. During this period her clients, including couture houses such as Givenchy and Chanel and designers such as Chloe, Matthew Williamson, Clements Ribeiro and John Rocha, have kept her continually busy. She finds that one of the main differences between producing ideas for fashion and those for interiors is that fashion has a much stronger narrative element. 'I trawl car boot sales constantly. One find was a gathered shiny rayon pillowcase, which inspired the designs I did with ruched satin flowers for a range called "Frida Kahlo meets Singapore Whore House" for Clements Ribeiro. Fashion designers have their own unique handwriting and I have to tailor my work to suit. They give completely different directions; some provide very detailed direction, with pictures and mood boards, whilst with others it may be just a word or two such as "something funky". I do

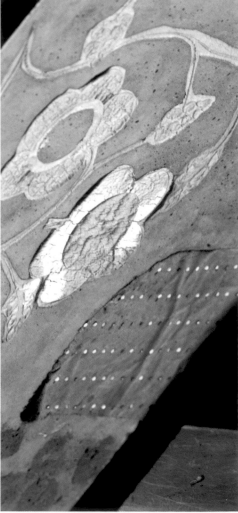

Patricia Belford was responsible for reintroducing the technique of devoré printing to the design industry, devoré being the erosion of one fibre from another. It is this technique that has inspired her investigations into patterning the surface of concrete, and an example of how processes can cross the boundaries between fashion fabrics and products for interiors. Textiles are embedded into the concrete and allowed to set for two weeks. Belford then abrades the surface to reveal the textile pattern imprinted beneath (opposite).

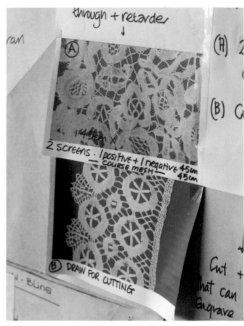

'Why not carve flowers on our buildings?'

Alain de Botton[7]

get wonderful design briefs that are really thrilling to work with. British designer Betty Jackson asked me to "imagine yourself on a railway station in the 1940s and it is damp and steamy and you notice a woman who is tearfully waving goodbye to her boyfriend who is going off to fight in the war. She is holding a bedraggled bunch of roses. I want those roses." Or another theme was "shabby circuses", where I embroidered satin to give the impression of it being worn over and over again.'

There is also the inspiration to be found in new techniques. 'Every season I try to find new ways of doing things, often the visual information I receive dictates the kind of stitch or technique I use.'

Patricia Belford also finds that exploring new techniques is inspirational. As co-founder of Belford Prints, one of the most successful specialized print companies in the UK, she has produced innovative textiles in collaboration with clients such as Vivienne Westwood, Donna Karan, Neisha Crosland

and Matthew Williamson. She explains the necessity for continual innovation, now that most of the manufacturing of textiles takes place in China. 'For example, when devoré lost its popularity in the late 1990s, the market became flooded once it was made so cheaply in China, and I had to find a replacement. I looked at ways of flocking, and invested a lot of money in some flocking machines. For a while I thought I had made a huge mistake, as initially developing the fabric for fashion, I realized that it had only a limited number of outlets. I produced a number of 33-foot (10-metre) lengths of a long pile flock for bags that taught me so much about the technique, knowledge that only really paid off when it started to be used by the interiors market and I began to get a return on the investment. Designing for interiors has more sustainability; it isn't feasible to spend a lot of time and money on sampling a fabric that will be out of date in six months, as it is in fashion. It's exhausting.'

Concrete curtains: the juxtaposition of hard-edged concrete with boudoir-like fringing by Girli Concrete™. The idea of the suburban net curtain is subverted here by layers of net laser-cut into a pattern and then sandwiched together to provide light with privacy.

Overleaf. A hard surface is softened by flocking – a short-cut pile – on the concrete, which Belford describes as 'like lichen on a rock face'. Flocked fabric 'Hortense' by Belford, commissioned by Designer's Guild for William Yeoward.

Belford's ability to innovate and push forward the boundaries of surface design has led to her present post as Senior Research Fellow at the University of Ulster in Northern Ireland. Together with Ruth Morrow, Professor of Architecture at the same institution, they are conducting research into the integration of textile technologies into the production of building products, such as concrete, one of the most widely used manmade substances throughout the world, and one with unfortunate connotations. Associated with the New Brutalism architecture of the 1960s, pock-marked and stained by the passage of time, concrete is being reassessed as being both fashionable and functional. Architects, engineers and designers are recognizing the potential of this manmade product to add warmth, texture and decorative detail to a room.

Belford and Morrow explain, 'Textiles are very often perceived as an addition to the inherent structure of an interior; Girli Concrete™ is born out of a larger drive to transform traditionally "hard" building products, defined by technical performance only, into innovative "soft" products that address both technical and human performance.' This process challenges the perception of textiles as only the 'dressing' to structure and instead integrates textile technologies into the actual building products. These 'low-tech' methods of wet and dry concrete casting with 'high-tech' textile methods of laser cutting/etching, flocking and digital printing transform a low-grade material into highly tactile, aesthetic products. Concrete and textile production are two of the principal traditional industries of Northern Ireland. As a reflection of this geographical heritage, the traditional textile crafts of the country, Irish lace and the Aran sweater, are being used as the visual inspiration for these building materials. Such innovation is an expensive and labour-intensive activity, only sustainable over the long term by developing products for both interiors and fashion.

Stripes are the most expedient way of arranging a series of colours that progress through the spectrum. Heti Gervis of product design and colour consultancy Hargreaves-Gervis lays out her colour palettes as a series of stripes that work coherently.

'Colours are not constants. They are subtle chameleons, taking on the character of the shapes, spaces and objects they occupy.'

Tricia Guild[8]

It is self-evident that colour is the single most important element of a design, coming before fabric, cut or embellishment, and conveying season, mood and style. In interiors colour sets the tone and mood of a room. The Institute of Contemporary Arts (ICA) reflects, 'Every spinner, weaver, fashion or interior designer and retailer knows the vital significance of colour to their business. But the key question they confront every season is which colour? Get the answer right and a product will sell to the next link in the textile chain. Getting it wrong means big trouble! In other words, in the twenty-first century, colour – above all other factors – means business.'

Designers of both fashion and interiors respond to the work of artists such as Yves Klein, Mark Rothko, Dan Flavin and Ellsworth Kelly, using their colour palette to inspire their collections. It is the knowledge of such upcoming exhibitions, as well as many other factors that lead the international colourists to decide on the directional colours 22 months ahead of the retailing season. Such is the rapidity of change that the creation of the bi-annual International Colour Authority palettes are now supplemented by a fortnightly online service from World Colour News offering the latest in global colour information, developments and products.

International colourist Heti Gervis suggests that the timescale may be much longer. 'Colours can take a surprisingly long time to come through,' she explains. 'It is at least six years since I first suggested teal, for instance, and it was only several seasons later that it began to be seen in fashion and interiors.' Together with business partner Alison Hargreaves they form product design and colour consultancy company Hargreaves-Gervis, which numbers American multinational company Gap as one of its many clients. Initially having trained as a textile designer, Gervis's approach to colour is developed out of her own personal aesthetic. 'I lay out my

Pages from the sketchbook of colourist Heti Gervis of Hargreaves-Gervis showing the development of a colour palette from the initial hand-mixed and painted colours in gouache to the final stripes. The company was one of the first to reintroduce highly coloured flock wallpaper, a technique that had previously been on the wane.

colour palettes as a series of stripes, and whereas a big company such as Trend Union might offer 50 new colours for the season for the designer to work from, I will give eight colours that all work together. My palettes tend to be used as a guide for the level of individual colour to be used in a collection, as well as the overall palette.'

While she cites travel and exhibitions as sources of inspiration she is not influenced by trends, although as she says, 'if you are thinking about it, then so are others. I am outside trends, but paradoxically, always in trend. Coming from an artistic point of view rather than having a "cool hunting", anthropological

approach, I put colours that go together, that look new, rather than saying, as the trend forecasters might, "this season it has to be red for this or that reason".'

There is now much less seasonality in colour palettes over the course of the year. According to Gervis, 'Colours used to be darker in fall and winter, but that is no longer the case. I do four colour palettes a year, and it takes me about three weeks to work out the direction in which I want to go; it is very challenging and instinctive. I look at things I like, such as 1960s American photography. Although the colour palette for interiors changes less quickly than that of fashion, the desire for change is accelerating. Fashion moves so quickly that a style can be in the shops in four weeks, and the mass market for interiors is catching up; there is much more colour in people's lives now, they are far more open to its possibilities. We produced a range of orange and duck-egg blue flock wallpaper several years ago, and it really kick-started the trend for highly coloured wallpaper.' She explains that she does not use any commercial colour systems, 'I hand mix my own colours, I don't use Pantone, my interest is in the relationship between colours and how they affect each other. It is a very personal process.'

Colour systems by companies such as Pantone are the preferred means of communicating accurate colour samples between designer, manufacturer, retailer and consumer. Their pens have been the favoured tool of fashion, textile and graphic designers since 1965, when the first Pantone matching system of artists' materials was launched. Now that the 1,932 colours of the Pantone Textile Color System are available, the accurate transition of a colour from paper to fabric is assured. Such is the close relationship between the colours for fashion and those used for interiors, that the paint manufacturer Crown now markets their colour palette with reference to the catwalk. Their paint colours are named 'eveningwear', 'corset', 'tailored' or 'crochet' and their

promotional literature is fronted with a quote from Professor Wendy Dagworthy, Head of the School of Fashion at London's Royal College of Art: 'The links between the fashion and interior design industry are now integral to modern-day living. It's well established that the international fashion catwalks have a direct influence on today's home interest trends but what has changed is how quickly these directions have an impact on the home – often less than six months, which is a fantastic opportunity for the consumer to chose from the very latest looks for their wardrobe as well as the way they transform their home.'

Dublin-born designer Orla Kiely, acknowledged globally for her unique, instantly recognizable print aesthetic and use of colour, includes the Dulux Design Council in her list of consultancies. 'Paint manufacturers are very aware of trends. As members of their creative board, we highlight global trends and suggest ways to move the colour palette forward.

Left. The Pantone colour system is a valuable tool for those designers who prefer to tap into a predicted format.

Opposite. Dublin-born designer Orla Kiely has her own very distinctive colour palette that renders her unique print designs instantly recognizable, as seen in her design studio.

The preliminary stages of the art work in the design studio of Oral Kiely and the final product on display in the shop.

Colour is an instinctive thing, but there are certain things I do recommend – not to combine lots of opposing brights for instance. It's imperative to work in tones and neutrals, to use something to bring the bright colour back "down", such as brown or a warm grey. When the general tone or mood of a season is sombre, flashes and accents of colour are very important to bring "up" the dark shades.'

The Orla Kiely label was launched in the 1990s with a small bag collection that has developed into a ready-to-wear women's line, menswear and products for the home. The simple leaf and stem design that forms the Orla Kiely logo represents the sources, simplicity and freshness of the designer's aesthetic. 'We are not trend driven, but every season we develop and push things further; it would be very boring to stick to the same thing. My taste has always been consistent, but I don't want to be stifled by it. The impulse to create is an instinct that most designers have; it is an ability to absorb,

without realizing, the things that provide new directions.' The designer attributes this instinct to being aware, not only of the usual visually influential exhibitions and films but also of the way life itself changes. 'An exhibition might kick-start an idea, but creativity is much more about the cultural context of design – an example is the contemporary desire to utilize every space in the home; even a shed in the garden is converted into a haven.' Geography also plays a part. 'People travel much more, and so are aware of other cultures, but context is important. Colour is enormously changeable in different lights, so sometimes colour palettes don't work internationally.'

The move into homeware was a logical progression. The designer explains, 'If you are interested in design and fashion you are going to take the same kind of approach to the home. If I love a print, I can make it work in all areas, even though on furniture it is static whereas fabric drapes around the body. Changing the

Orla Kiely

scale of a design has interesting results, and an exaggeratedly big scale is always impactful.' In developing her ideas, Kiely recognizes the importance of being open to change. 'We are all exposed constantly to so many new things in life, that we are instilled with the need to change. Obviously in interiors this can be a huge investment, but even so, there is the same keenness that there is in fashion to constantly refresh.'

Inspiration comes in many guises; it is never just about a colour, a trend, a texture or a form. It might be mediated through technological processes or cultural configurations; how it occurs is, to those who lack it, a mystery. However it is defined, it is certain that its presence fuels creative activity on a global scale.

Discreet touches of the print on the clutch bag are enough to identify the Orla Kiely aesthetic in her fashion collection.

Good taste is not an absolute; it all depends on context. Designers are subject to changes in taste and yet remain responsible for them, a paradox that leads to consensus. The move away from minimalism is providing a new design aesthetic for the twenty-first century, that of eclecticism, where designers play with the concept of taste in a mood of irony or self-conscious kitsch, whilst still retaining a reverence for craftsmanship and originality. Design in a postmodern context is no longer about simple problem solving, but about creating the covetable. Changes in taste occur frequently, good taste is a relative concept, and is to do with how, when and where we live.

This has not always been the case. The term 'good taste' meaning 'sound understanding' appears in the early fifteenth century, but it was not until the eighteenth century that taste became synonymous with judgment,[1] at a time when art was no longer perceived as divinely inspired but was fast becoming a commodity, and subject to the whims of the consumer.

Good taste was initially thought to be the prerogative of the visually literate. One of the processes of initiation for those in pursuit of this understanding was the 'Grand Tour', a journey of some months undertaken by youthful European aristocrats from the seventeenth century. These excursions into culture lasted until the advent of mass rail travel at the beginning of the twentieth century. Once the masses could access these treasures, they ceased to have such significance for the upper classes. The purpose of the tour was primarily educational, to expose the young mind to the artefacts of antiquity and the Renaissance and thus to further their understanding and appreciation of beauty. It also became an opportunity to purchase fine art and objects to be displayed on their return. Good taste was subsequently seen as an

'Taste is individual choice, which has nothing to do with good or bad taste.'

Gijs Bakker, Droog Design[2]

Kitchens have traditionally been associated with 'white goods', the kitchen a scientific arena and white being perceived as hygienic. The applied decoration on this cloisonné washing machine by electronics manufacturer JL recognizes that the kitchen is now considered another room, rather than just a place to prepare food, and that appliances have become another opportunity to embrace a lifestyle product.

Above. Regent Street looking south from the Hanover Chapel, 1842, by Thomas Shotter Boys from the publication *Original Views of London*. Many department stores, such as London's Harrods and Le Bon Marché in Paris, were established during the nineteenth century as shopping became a fashionable activity.

Opposite. In nineteenth-century Britain, the influence of the Grand Tour receded and mass consumption conversely exploded, with the manufacture of overwrought, highly decorated machine-made artefacts for the Victorian interior proliferating to ghastly excess.

absolute, rooted in the informed choice of the select few, and the direct result of an education in the aesthetics of the period.

The democratization of taste began in the twentieth century, when the economy was transformed by the manufacture and retailing of products through industrial progress and invention, efficient methods of supply and developments in retail strategies. The concomitant increase in the standard of living was a reflection of this and resulted in the rise of the European and American department store. By the late nineteenth century, Paris, London, Berlin, Brussels, Vienna and Milan all offered city sites as a focus for sartorial experimentation and social display.[3]

Women's greater social freedom and a more efficient transport system meant that for the first time shopping became a leisure activity. Purchasing luxury commodities for the home, together with the wearing of fashionable dress, was an opportunity to convince less fortunate competitors

in a society driven by capitalism of the thrilling purchasing power of new money.

Western society was hot to shop, and questions about what was made, bought and sold, began to concern social reformers such as Britain's Sir Henry Cole. A leading member of the commission that organized 'The Great Exhibition of the Works of Industry of All Nations' held in London's Hyde Park in 1851, Cole saw an opportunity to engage the masses in a dialogue of what constituted 'good taste'. His desire was to unite the practice of fine art with industry. This led to the burgeoning of the practice of industrial design; he created a syllabus in British art and design colleges that is still relevant today, and that became the paradigm for design education around the world. Such a system is responsible for the cross-fertilization of ideas between the disciplines of fine art, textiles, graphics, product design, fashion design, jewelry making and ceramics that informs much of contemporary European design practice.

Similarly, China, which is keen to have a few brands of its own, is developing an art and design programme to provide design skills; the country seeks to replace 'Made in China' with 'Designed in China'. Their current teaching strategies provide the technical skills, but not the ability, to work across disciplines. Their programmes are very often set up and assessed by staff from British art and design colleges.

In a society where artefacts are bought rather than inherited, taste is a consumer-driven construct, and inextricably bound up with notions of class; the desire to consume deemed an activity of the acquisitive middle classes, with status marked by novelty rather than longevity. Previously, only the aristocrat could afford to buy or commission furniture, but once the middle classes had access to new things, the demarcation lines had to be redrawn between the two. The upper classes withdrew their patronage from the furniture makers and their skills – a form of snobbery that still survives

today in the damning remark that 'He is the sort who has to buy his own furniture'.

The desire for contemporary furniture accelerated in the 1960s with the enormous shifts in postwar life. The universal desire to embrace the new at a time of unprecedented affluence resulted in entrepreneurial activities in all aspects of design. Italy, in particular, during the period between 1945 and 1965 (now known as the Ricostruzione), was developing a design industry that was to influence the world, and make household names of fashion designer Emilio Pucci and product designer Gio Ponti. Piero Busnelli founded his first company producing armchairs in 1953, but it was not until 1966, and his development, production and application of a cold framed polyurethane process to furniture making, that he started large-scale mass production. In 1966 he founded C&B Italia with Cesare Cassina, and in 1973 took over the company and renamed it B&B Italia, now a multi-million-pound global furniture business.

Channelling the psychedelic moulded plastic furniture design of Verner Panton of the 1960s, the chaise longue 'Fly' by B&B Italia SpA reflects the ongoing preoccupation by designers and manufacturers with the innovations, colours, materials and forms of that decade.

Sheridan Coakley puts the pivotal date for the consumer's desire for modern furniture as being somewhat later; he has been manufacturing furniture by designers such as Jasper Morrison and Matthew Hilton since the opening of his London flagship store SCP in 1985. 'The desire for contemporary furniture started in the 1980s; modern design is now the norm, whereas before it was considered nouveau. People then were only interested in buying traditional or antique pieces, and I sold mostly to architects or the contract market. Modern architecture means that the function of our furniture has changed; sofas no longer have to have high backs for instance, because of draughts. We no longer trade off nostalgia; we are now a modern society.'

The Great Exhibition was a didactic exercise to educate consumers through exposure to the best and worst the world's manufacturers had to offer. A similar attempt to inspire discrimination in the consumer was undertaken in 1909 by Gustav Pazaurek, director of the Industrial Museum in Stuttgart, where he created his 'Museum of Art Indiscretions'. Under the heading 'Bad Taste' the catalogue includes such things as 'China flower vases in the form of hollowed-out tree trunks.'[5] What he would have made of the ceramic teddy bears of Swedish designer Bodil Soderlund, a perfect example of kitsch, we can only speculate.

Kitsch is an almost inevitable consequence of using an inappropriate material; in the case of the teddy bears their function is to comfort and soothe infants, an impossible requirement of porcelain's fragile yet resisting surface. However, this is not to damn the teddy bears as 'poor taste', since kitsch relies almost entirely for its impact on context and a knowing appreciation of its meaning. In this case, the artist is concerned to show how the teddy bear transcends its childhood resonance and becomes a reliquary of youthful memories. Geography also plays a part. To find a ceramic teddy bear in some small craft pottery in the

'I'd like to see designers come up with a new vocabulary of ornament.'

Joseph Holtzman, founder and editor of *Nest*[4]

Opposite. A metallic horse from the menagerie of American designer Jonathan Adler. His manifesto rejoices in the death of minimalism; 'We believe in irreverent luxury and that your home should make you happy'.

Right. The precepts that form follows function and that decoration is somehow less than cerebral has meant that patterned and printed fabrics for upholstery have generally been considered evidence of bad taste. This contemporary version of a toile de Jouy by textile design company Timorous Beasties, founded in 1990 by Alistair McAuley and Paul Simmons, covers the 'Elsie' sofa designed by Russell Pinch for furniture company SCP, showing that print and pattern are once again desirable aesthetics.

The London store Vessel also provides gallery space to showcase the work of contemporary designers such as Aldo Londi Bitossi, whose ceramic cats (opposite) inject wit and humour into the traditional idea of an 'ornament'.

middle of the countryside or on the shelves of a shop selling tourist memorabilia will evoke a different response in us from when it is viewed in a sophisticated urban gallery space. Appreciating kitsch implies a 'knowingness', an attitude that is a direct outcome of postmodernism, in itself a reaction to modernism, in which everything is thought to be equal in value, that the beauty of a piece is not dependent on craftsmanship or skill of execution, but with its impact on the viewer or purchaser.

As individuals we like to hold ourselves as a sort of benchmark – he has bad taste, while I am aware of the nuances of irony. It may be considered superficial to judge people on the evidence of their taste, but it is an inevitable consequence of living in a society where we buy what we like, rather than what we need. Once choice comes into play our purchases reflect both our lifestyle and our aspirations; that both may be found wanting by an interested observer is a risk we take in exercising that

choice, although making such judgments with confidence has become increasingly complex in these postmodern times. This multiplicity of choice means that there is no longer one acceptable visual style for either interiors or fashion, as evidenced by the eclectic nature of the catwalk collections and the many 'lifestyle' choices on offer from various big name brands.

In contemporary society good taste may be perceived as an outdated concept, shorthand to visual acceptability for those who lack imagination. Where once we derided interiors filled with 'knick-knacks' (defined by the Oxford English dictionary as 'a small worthless object, especially an ornament') and 'clutter' from the vantage point of late twentieth-century neomodernism, there is now a plethora of products that celebrate the re-emergence of the ornament, such as the whimsical vintage towelling soft toys by Thorsten van Elten and the animal figurines of Aldo Londi-Bitossi.

Decorative accessories as 'conversation pieces':
a hippopotamus plate by radical Dutch designer
Hella Jongerius, a bird bowl by American designer
Jonathan Adler and glass birds by Oiva Toikka.

Taste is all to do with context, and when the 'must have' designer handbag started toting a cluster of whimsical charms, and accessories began to have their own accessories (Louis Vuitton, Prada and Miu Miu all produce quirky little things to attach to an attaching device that in turn attaches them to the handbag or phone), it was representative of the fashionable trend for pleasure in the purposeless of *things*, what design historian Stephen Bayley describes as 'feckless neophilia, a restless quest for novelty cynically separated from purpose or need.'[6] Further customizing a bag with trinkets and devices that already bears a much coveted logo is a way of personalizing the precious, and injecting some levity into the seriousness of the style statement, a concept that has been quick to translate into objects for interiors. Ornaments, too, deflect the worthiness of an iconic piece of furniture, and allow for a sense of fun to intrude on what might be a clinical, almost curatorial space.

Angel Monzon is art director and co-owner of Vessel, a store and gallery situated in London's Notting Hill that specializes in the work of the new avant-garde designers. 'When I started Vessel seven years ago the intention was to concentrate on design classics, in line with Walter Gropius's definition of good design that it should have beauty, quality, function and affordability. We would have been embarrassed to describe an object as decorative. All that has changed, and in the last four years decoration has been creeping in.' Monzon relates this to the influence of fashion. 'It started in fashion, this desire for the decorative, birds, butterflies and flowers. Then it moved into wallpapers and textiles, and finally it has gone into 3D.'

Featuring the work of designers such as The Netherlands' Hella Jongerius, Spanish born Jaime Hayon and Finland's Oiva Toikka, the gallery celebrates the appeal of the ornament. 'People use decoration in a very different way to the previous

Spanish designer Jaime Hayon crosses the boundaries between art, design and craft and introduces traditional artisanal skills to produce quirky yet voluptuous ceramics. The high gloss of the surface of the horse's head and the space between the ears for flowers results in a sensual and dramatic wall decoration. The same pursuit of the idiosyncratic can be seen in his designs for the Camper shoe store (opposite); new technologies were deployed in the manufacture of the whimsical multi-legged cabinet and red reflective floor.

generation; it is not like the clutter of our grandparents' homes. It is much more considered, and a juxtaposition of different styles. Now I feel it is more important to tell a story, to have a relationship with the object. People are in love with the figurine.'

Jaime Hayon trained as an industrial designer in Madrid, before heading the design department of Italian fashion house Benetton's Communication and Fine Arts Foundation in northern Italy from 1997 to 2004, curating exhibitions and holding workshops. In 2002 he won the INJUVE (Ministry of Culture) award for Spain's most promising designer, and his latest role is as art director of porcelain company Lladro. His witty and irreverent work breaks down the barriers between art, craft and design. The contemporary desire for eclecticism and the referencing of differing historical styles is amply demonstrated by his bright blue Multileg cabinet, which features legs from a multiplicity of historical periods: Louis XIV, Art Deco, the Bauhaus. Alice

Rawsthorne, design critic of the *International Herald Tribune* places him in the context of the current debate about the ephemeral nature of contemporary design. 'In the early Noughties design was dominated by fairytale romanticism. Since then a group of European designers has emerged with an exuberant neo-baroque visual language that mixes product, interior and graphic design. We live in a post-industrial culture in which most objects have been reinvented so often that it's becoming harder for designers to improve upon existing types. That's why product designers like Jaime are increasingly using graphic design to make their work seem fresh.' Zeev Aram, who held a retrospective of Hayon's work in 2006, thinks a sense of humour for a designer is essential. 'Good design is associated with sombreness, but it is very, very important that the designer also has a sense of humour, even though he or she must be serious about what they do.'

Trends in fashion and interiors now have a commonality, though they may go

Above. The chandelier, whether antique or a historical pastiche, such as this one in black crystal by French product designer Philippe Starck, is ubiquitous in the contemporary interior.

Above right. Belgian-born designer Dries Van Noten has an aesthetic far removed from minimalism, being concerned with rich embellishment and the layering of many and various print techniques.

Opposite. Neither a bedchamber nor a dressing room, the boudoir was historically a very specific social space, which, by the mid-eighteenth century, had evolved into a luxuriously decorated sitting room. The modern interpretation is one of lush textures, a predilection for animal print and sumptuous adornment.

by a different name. What is 'vintage' in fashion is described as 'the new antiques' in furniture, a title appropriated by designer Marcel Wanders. Just as there is a limit to the number of vintage garments to be found and manufacturers have had to replicate the look of iconic pieces to fulfil an ever-increasing demand, so it is with the remaking of classic pieces of furniture such as the world's first cantilevered chair made from a single piece of plastic by Verner Panton.

An example of this confluence in trends is that of the baroque opulence of 'boudoir chic' in interiors that occurred at the beginning of the twenty-first century, and the sustained popularity of a look in fashion exemplified by designers such as Dries Van Noten; one of lavish layered embellishment. This move towards decadence and luxury was epitomized by the advertisement for the Gucci pochette, the bag set down amongst cigarette ends and empty champagne glasses. Professor Caroline Cox of the

University of the Arts, London and author of *Seduction* describes this style as 'the triumph of the feminine decorative over masculinist modernist austerity. The French rococo motif and boudoir aesthetic is completely female, and this is perceived as trivial, overblown and sexy. It was a look invented for women.' Adolf Loos certainly considered that the womanly desire for adornment placed her at the lower end of civilization. 'Freedom from ornament is a sign of spiritual strength,' he wrote in his defining essay 'Ornament and Crime' in 1908, and that with female economic independence 'velvet and silk, flowers and ribbons, feathers and paint will fail to have their effect.'[7]

This explosion of fashion into texture and colour that occurred at the beginning of the twenty-first century resonated with a reappraisal of the mannered extravagance of Paul Poiret, a couturier from the beginning of the century before, who instigated one of the first attempts at 'folk' dress. It is now the late Cristóbal Balenciaga and his

A significant move towards the new silhouette, French-born designer Roland Mouret's 'Galaxy' dress.

concern with architectural simplicity that is providing inspiration, at the couture house Balenciaga, fronted by Nicolas Ghesquière. There is a shift in emphasis away from decorative excesses towards a new version of modernism, a more organic and streamlined approach, evidenced by the emergence of the Roland Mouret 'Galaxy' dress, a name that resonates with visions of the 1950s space race and the desire for modernism.

This style statement marked the beginning of playing with form and structure and the return to volume in fashion, evidenced in the work of designers such as Alber Elbaz for Lanvin. Embellishment exists in the accessories. The architectonic structure of these monumental clothes is worn with quirky and extravagantly figured bags and shoes of such idiosyncratic complexity that they become less an accessory and more a fact. Miu Miu's cherry patent shoes have gilded, carved wooden soles decorated with rococo flourishes and a high riveted strap across the instep. A visual culture that accommodates the juxtaposition of this embellished and over-ornamented shoe, the understated luxury of an Armani interior, the porcelain horse's head by Jaime Hayon and a monumental trapeze coat from Nicolas Ghesquière is one where 'good taste' has no meaning; there is only the discriminating 'eye'.

'Most of us live in homes that evolve and grow as we do, and changing as our life changes rather than as fashions do. But we should not underestimate the effect that fashion and trends and technology have on our lives.'

Stafford Cliff [8]

Customer requirements increasingly extend beyond the purchase of new products to demanding advice on how to put them together. Armani is one of the labels increasingly diversifying into furniture, tableware, linens and rugs who also offers a personalized interior décor service and made-to-measure facility for those customers who wish to embrace the lifestyle of understated luxury that is the Armani Casa brand.

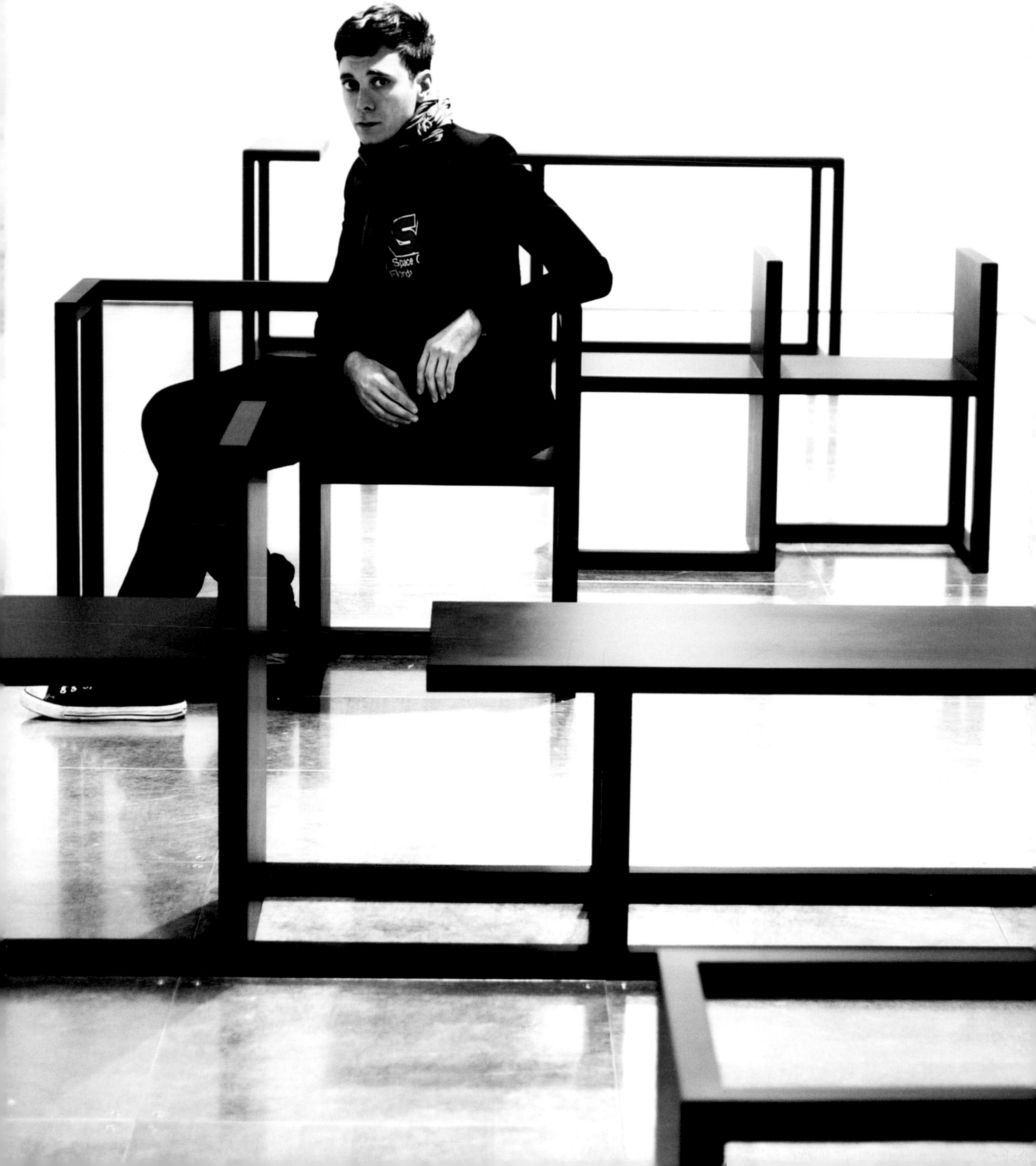

Page 86. French couturier Cristóbal Balenciaga was renowned for the dramatic use of volume and the sculptural cut of his clothes. As the current creative director of the house, Nicolas Ghesquière continues this tradition with his modern aestheticism.

Page 87. The minimalistic and pared-down style established by French designer Hedi Slimane during his time at the French couture house Dior Homme is reflected here in his furniture.

Left. It is rare for textile and wallpaper designers to have the opportunity to realize their designs into a finished interior. Here, Neisha Crosland's aesthetic is incorporated into the interior of the reception room at Eton Place, London.

The role of the decorator

One of the major differences between designing for interiors and designing for fashion is control over the end product. Although to a certain extent fashion has become celebrity led, and thus much influenced by fashion stylists such as Rachel Zoe, currently considered by Tom Ford to be one of the most influential people in American fashion, interiors are mediated through the decorator, a profession that was barely accepted as legitimate before World War II.

Fashion stylists are a relatively new phenomenon; in part the outcome of sartorial disasters by actors on the Oscar red carpet. Although stylists now permeate all aspects of the fashion industry, from marketing a brand to organizing advertorial and editorial photographic shoots, it is still the customer who chooses the clothes. Neisha Crosland explains, 'With fashion you offer a whole look, it's all worked out, whereas interior decorators come into the shop with their own ideas of how to use my fabrics; I'm selling swatches to the furniture world. In the US you cannot buy a length of fabric anywhere unless you are a decorator and have trade references, that is why my shop is not a showroom, I want my work to be accessible to all, even if the customer only requires a cushion.' Julius Walters of the silk-weaving company Stephen Walters and Sons is also convinced of the importance of the decorator. 'The decorator has a big role to play in the furnishings market, just as we are reliant on the fashion designer to use our fabrics.'

Celia Birtwell concurs. An iconic print designer for fashion in the 1960s, she subsequently designed fabrics for interiors. Now once again designing much sought-after fashion ranges for the British high-street store Topshop, she has experience of both aspects of the market. 'Rooms are to do with one's personality and good decorators can apply that personality to a place. The frustrating thing about designing home textiles is that your fabrics go off on a roll and are made up by somebody else and you never see where they land. With fashion you'll see someone tripping down the street wearing something that you've done and you can think that looks nice or dreadful or whatever but you don't have that joy with fabrics for the home. In order to understand interior textiles, you need to put them on a product because the sad truth is that a lot of people don't have an eye or a vision.'[9]

America was the first country to embrace the notion of 'interior design', an activity far removed from simply choosing

Textile designer Celia Birtwell and fashion designer Ossie Clark offered a triumphant synthesis of garment and pattern during the 1960s and 1970s. Subsequently Birtwell concentrated on fabrics for interiors, before reclaiming her fashion customers with a sell-out range for British high-street retailers Topshop (left). The fabric, 'Beasties', is from her contemporary couture collection.

Overleaf. Celia Birtwell fabrics are hand-printed in England.

Opposite. A new eclecticism in interiors emerged at the beginning of the twenty-first century. It accommodates the incorporation of antique furniture in a playful irreverent way that imbues the notion of theatricality into the home.

Above. The Colony Club at 120 Madison Avenue, New York, was the first major interior design commission for Elsie de Wolfe. Her precepts included a respect for the past, 'beautiful things are faithful friends, and they stay beautiful, they become more beautiful as they get older', diluted with a practical approach to modernism. 'The most important thing in designing furniture – or anything we use – are the three genies of the fairy whose name is Good Taste, and they're called "Simplicity", "Suitability," and "Proportion".'[10]

the colour of the paint and hanging the curtains. The rise of the new middle classes during the nineteenth century revealed a populace defeated by the amount of choice on offer from a newly industrialized society turning out heavy 'brown' furniture in High Victorian style. It was inevitable that an industry would arise out of the need to pare down these horrors in keeping with the burgeoning modern movement, which arose after World War I. The Victorian desire for stuff was about the insecurities of the nouveau riche. Postwar, such preoccupations with lavish display seemed misplaced. The first to exploit this requirement was, by her own admission, Elsie de Wolfe. 'I think I may say that I created the profession of interior decorator. I may also say that I rescued the American house and made it liveable. I opened the doors of the American house, and the windows, and let in the air and the sunshine. Up to then everything was closed, and people never used what they

called the parlour in their houses, and the furniture was sentimental and gloomy, and doom hung in the rooms where it stood.' Elsie de Wolfe's juxtaposition of historical artefacts and modern interiors remains seductive. Her aesthetic is still absolutely in tune with the twenty-first-century vogue for eclecticism. 'Louis Quatorze, Louis Quinze and Seize, became my loves. I am accused of having made America conscious of antiques…good antiques live very happily with modern things, and especially against modern backgrounds.'[11]

Preoccupations with what our clothes and the interiors of our homes say about our personal sense of style remain paramount, and involve the desire of the consumer to be included with those 'in the know'. Access to fashion stylists and interior decorators both feed on the desire of being seen to 'get it'. Contemporary culture seems to value style above intelligence or generosity of spirit; it is therefore inevitable that confidence in one's place in the world is predicated on

A shoot for British fashion company Whistles and
an armchair from London-based antique dealers
Plinth reflect a concurrent mood in fashion and
interiors of an eclectic richly textured surface that
acknowledges the past but is intrinsically modern.

having an 'eye', even if that sensibility is
mediated through the decorator or through
appropriating the aesthetic of a brand.

Giorgio Armani pointed out in an
interview given at the opening of the first
Armani/Casa homewares store in London's
Bond Street in 2005. 'The next big thing in
luxury interior style will be a trend towards
customization. We all want to make our
houses personal to ourselves. My Armani/
Casa interior design service is a made-to-
measure service where the Armani style
does not dominate, but rather interacts
with the customer's own personality.' The
customer, however, will already be familiar
with the 'Armani look', and will hardly
expect any surprises on entering the store.
As designer Orla Kiely says, 'A consumer
lacking in confidence trusts a brand to make
their decisions for them. Their feeling is,
if they are showing it, it must be good.'

Interior designer Andrée Putman
points out the pitfalls of the profession.
'A home project depends enormously on
the personality of the client I am working
for, and some of them depress me very
much. They want to intimidate, to clearly
announce to the world that they've
achieved what they want to, and they use
their apartment like a kind of power.'[12]
Stephen Bayley concurs with his assertion
that 'interior design is a business whose
substance is a subterfuge; it derives
its character from historical ignorance
and its status from social fear.'[13]

Large-scale interior design projects
inevitably require a project manager and
the financial budget will reflect that, but
such autonomy for the designer does not
automatically result in an aesthetically
pleasing interior or one that appeals to
the emotions. When clients buy a couture
garment for a very large sum of money, they
are assured of exquisite craftsmanship but,
more particularly, iconoclastic design.
Moreover, the couture jacket may be
worn with a pair of jeans and tousled
hair, the evening dress with an old

mackintosh, new is worn with old, and the expensive with the mass-produced.

This is not always true of the work of the decorator, when such large amounts of money may mean lavish banality, if not over-designed frightfulness, where ludicrous and elaborate place settings, complicated soft furnishings and contrived eclectic collections of 'things' all go to create an environment that is far removed from the idea of 'home,' and where the incumbent must observe certain rules. Anarchy is not in the remit of the designed home; woe betide the minor maladjustment of a row of identical containers, or the casual strewing of the detritus of everyday life. As Andrée Putman says, 'There is something ambiguous about interior design; ways to do something that can look very dramatic – repetitions of the same idea for instance – and you think that's art. But it's not art.'[14]

The expression 'matchy-matchy' is used in fashion to describe over-organized outfits; bags matching shoes matching hat matching handbag matching gloves etc. The same principle can apply to interiors, and it is one that is far removed from the process of making personal choices about colour, texture, pattern and scale, and how we use the spaces in our homes. As the now Dowager Duchess of Devonshire remarked on being told to get a decorator on moving into Chatsworth House, one of Britain's grandest stately homes, 'I pondered the idea, but not for long. This house has so strong an atmosphere I felt it would be difficult for a stranger to get the feel of it, and I did not fancy being surrounded by someone else's taste.'[15]

The Blue Drawing Room at the ancestral seat of the Dukes of Devonshire, Chatsworth House, Derbyshire. The quintessence of English country house style: opulence tempered by the informality of chintz-covered comfortable furniture, flowers and an eclectic range of pictures including *The Acheson Sisters* by John Singer Sargent.

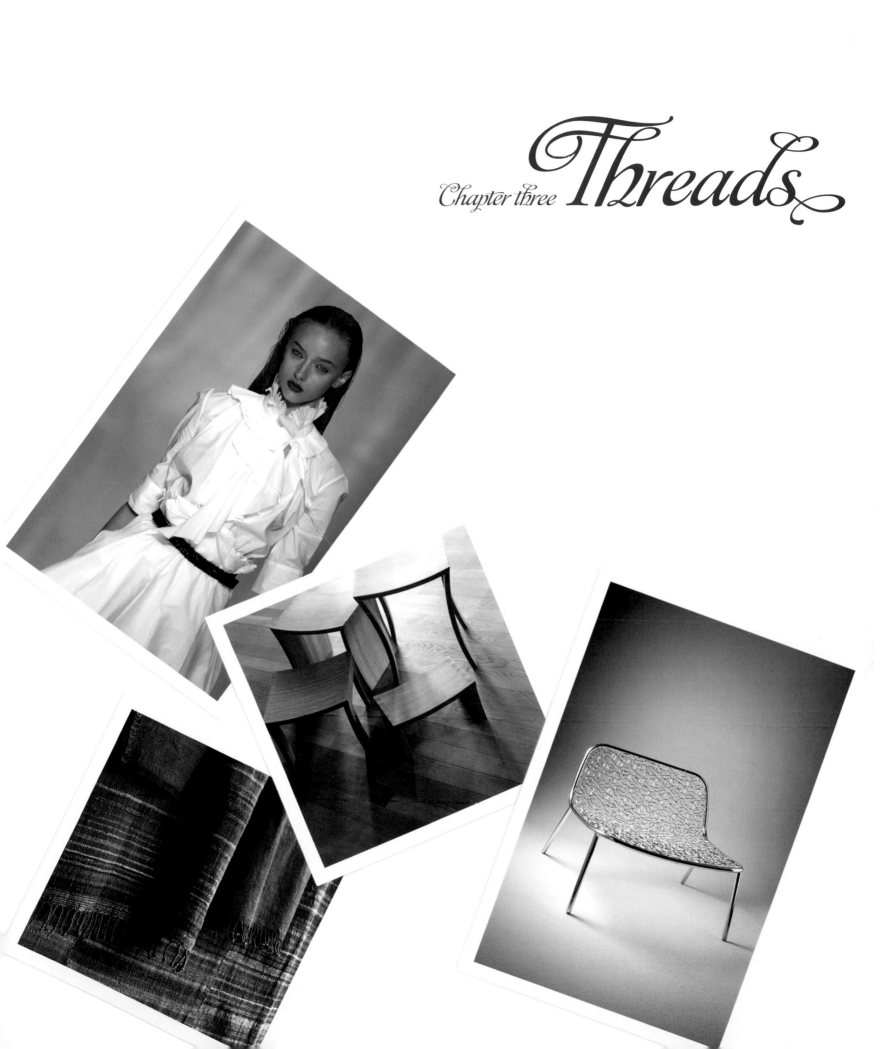

In the twenty-first century it is possible to observe an upsurge in the use of pattern, prints and textures that embraces all aspects of fashion and interiors, from wall coverings, fabric and furniture to products and accessories. Innovations in materials and processes are challenging designers to exploit to the full the potential of colour, pattern, surface and print. Many design practitioners produce weave and print ideas for fashion usage that 'travel' between products as diverse as sunglasses and luggage to wallpaper and chairs. Despite adopting their design aesthetic across a broad range of materials, the signature style of the designer remains constant.

This is particularly true of Italian design company Etro. Alongside Missoni and Versace, Etro is one of those companies comprised of family dynasties that seem to be a uniquely Italian phenomenon. Established in 1968 by founder and president Gimmo Etro the company was initially a manufacturer of prêt-à-porter and couture luxury fabrics in cashmere, linen and silk. In 1988 the label emerged into the fashion market with its own prêt-à-porter range of men's and women's wear, and in 1990 the first home collection was introduced.

Both the fashion and homeware collections reflect the company's heritage of luxury fibres and richly textured fabrics, particularly in the use of the paisley motif, which in 1981 became a symbol of the Etro label, an image redolent with overtones of a certain romantic bohemianism, albeit allied to craftsmanship and luxury. The paisley motif is one of the most enduring inspirations for the textile designer. Sometimes thought to be the mark made by curling the hand into the fist and printing with the little finger downwards into the cloth, the motif of the comma-shaped cone could also be interpreted as a seed pod and as such a symbol of life and fertility. Although the essential elements of the motif are always evident, designers over the ages have exaggerated

'Fashion is not something that exists only in dresses. Fashion is in the sky, in the street, in the way we live.'
Coco Chanel

Etro's origins as a fabric manufacturer is reflected in the importance invested in the quality of cloth in both the fashion and the homeware ranges, from the ornamental slippers to handbags and headscarves.

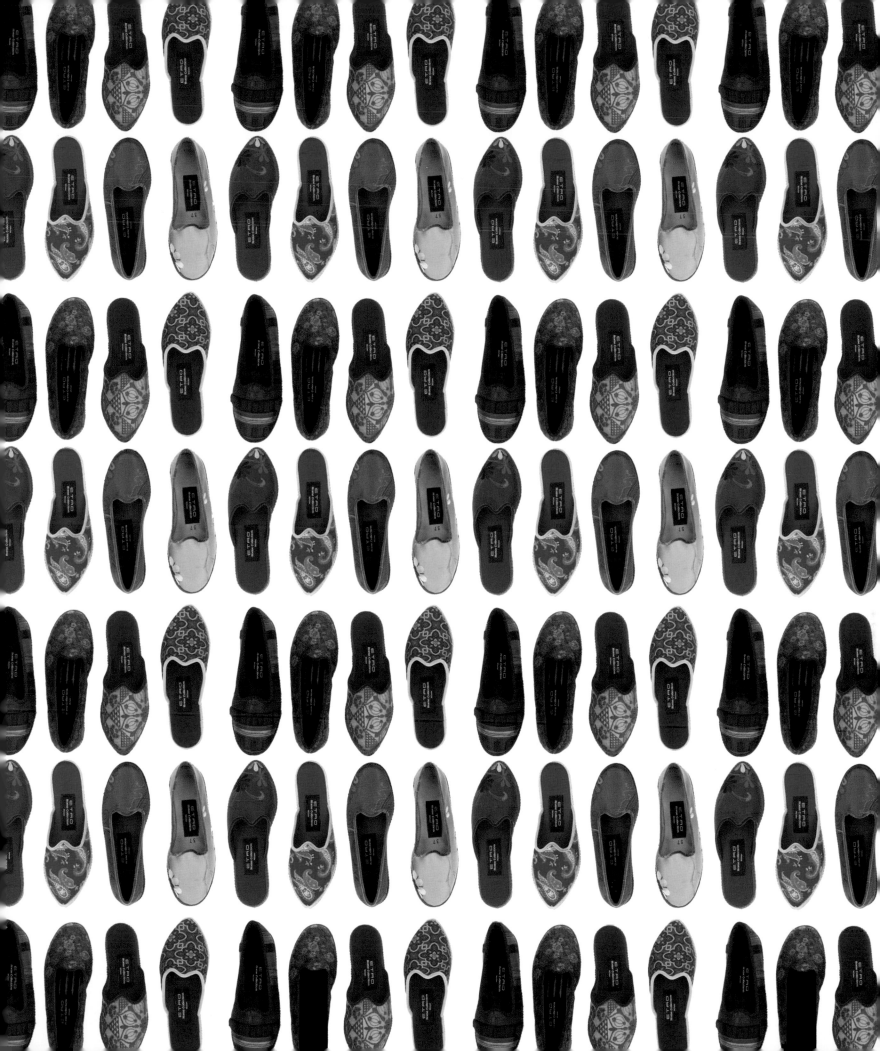

The subtlety of the colour and the intricacy of the surface pattern in these prints by Etro are typical of the label. The quality of a print may be defined by the number of screens used in its production. Sophisticated hues and tones in a design require countless colour separations (each colour needs a separate screen), which are both costly and labour intensive.

Eley Kishimoto demonstrates how scale is of paramount importance in designing prints that work both on the body and in interiors as one surface is static, the other animated.

and distorted the basic scroll-shaped unit and introduced variations in the length and scale of the fruit and the stalk. This means that the motif lends itself to use in both fashion and interiors, a fact that Etro has exploited in the 'New Traditions' range, which was introduced in 1994 and continues to be the cornerstone of the label.

Mark Eley and Wakako Kishimoto started the design label Eley Kishimoto in 1992, and their incisive and intelligent approach to print design placed them in the forefront of the subsequent reappraisal of the use of printed textiles for both interiors and fashion. Their distinctive work can be seen on the catwalk at their own-label twice-yearly collections in Paris, as well as in the collections of fashion luminaries such as Alexander McQueen, Marc Jacobs and Louis Vuitton. Their exuberant and adroit deployment of pattern and colour lends itself to a multiplicity of uses; the iconic 'Flash' design, based on an animal print, has become an enduring design classic that

Surface treatments of the cloth deploying unexpected materials and unusual components, such as flattened strips of fabric and raffia by couture embroiderer Karen Nicol, bring a new perspective to traditional embroidery skills.

is equally striking as wallpaper, furniture or on a garment. Mark Eley explains, 'we cross disciplines, but fundamentally we decorate the surface, enjoying other people's mediums. We do not design within other people's design disciplines.'

Not only can one design be used through different media, techniques themselves such as knitting, crochet, weaving and embroidery may also cross the boundaries of conventional usage. Swedish designer Moa Jantze embroiders a black-painted MDF rocking chair, inspired by a nineteenth-century quilt pattern, and radical Dutch designer Hella Jongerius uses threads in all sorts of contexts, including holes punched into ceramics and threaded through with bright embroidery silks.

Karen Nicol specializes in Irish, Cornelly, multihead machine, beading and hand embroidery. Her small atelier in London can produce up to one thousand fashion pieces a season for the top end of the market. She says, 'embroidery for couture

often stays in Europe, whilst embroidery for the mass market is done in India or China. At first quality was an issue, but now that has changed, and they can charge very low prices for beautiful embroidery. They don't yet, though, have the design skills that suit the western market, so that although I might do the design, the production may be sourced elsewhere. However, we still produce embroidery for the couture end of the market, and I do the catwalk shows.' This involves up to 30 pieces for each designer's show, sometimes with the addition of three copies of everything to go to America, Japan and Europe. Although there is a move towards more structured pieces in fashion, there remains a desire for the embellishment of cloth, but used in a different way – as an accent in a collection rather than overall.

The designer sees this trend permeating across the boundaries of fashion into interiors. 'I am now finding that there is a place for embellishment in interiors.

Decorators can sometimes be accused of putting together room sets that are a bit too tasteful and bland, and the rooms really need the addition of something distressed or edgy. I'm making very lush and extravagantly beaded and embroidered throws, "eveningwear for the sofa" I call them, supplying the same desire for the specialist couture one-off that I've been doing for fashion.' Nicol also designs and produces embroidered horsehair for furnishing textiles for clients such as Clarence House and Zimmer Rhode and has done pieces for the Wynne Hotel in Las Vegas, King Gustav of Sweden, the Thai Royal family and the King of Norway.

Knitted textiles are now used across a broad spectrum of products, from garments to furniture and furnishings. Added to the familiar hand knitting activity and work done on small domestic machines, are new industrial processes that provide unlimited potential in the development of fabrics for both interiors and fashion. Traditionally,

'warp' knitting, a cross between knitting and weaving where a warp of many threads creates vertical chains linked together, has been used for furnishing fabrics and 'weft' knitting, where a thread interloops through horizontal rows, has been used for clothing. 'Weft' knitting is more resilient and has greater design possibilities than 'warp' knitting. Knitted structures are an area where technology and design are inextricably linked, and innovations such as the 'single thread' garment, in which the product is knitted in one continuous piece, are now produced by mainstream manufacturers such as British company John Smedley. A similar vein of technology has been used extensively to produce three-dimensional seating forms in the automotive and contract furnishings industries.

The flexibility of the structure and the diversity of the knitting processes make the looped stitch uniquely suited to encompassing a variety of shapes, often with a playful eye. British *Vogue* features

Hilary Anderson-Barr uses traditional craft techniques in unexpected ways with her knitted vessels. Shown here is a hand-knitted 'Water Pitcher' vessel in natural Jacob yarn and small bowls in cream merino wool. (Bill Batten, *House and Garden* copyright The Conde Nast Publications Ltd.)

Opposite. Dressmaking techniques that are used to shape a garment also have their uses in the construction of furniture. Smocking allows for the suppression and expansion of fabric, creating fullness and tension that is sustained by the steel infrastructure of this chair by designer Patricia Urquiola for Moroso SpA.

Above. Marcel Wanders's knotted rope chair for Cappellini is resonant of the Indian charpoy day bed in that it allows a free flow of air around the body.

a cable-stitched car by Dream cars in a fashion shoot, and American *Vogue* pays homage to Canadian artist Janet Morgan with their set by Andy Hillman for an interview with Christopher Bailey in which every surface is clothed with knitted fabrics, from the television to the cup and saucer. British designer Hilary Anderson-Barr modifies knitted textiles to form textured vases. Her intention is to raise the perception of knitting as a craft by associating it with the art of the potter. She produces knitted vessels that mirror the style and design of ceramics; from a classical Greek amphora to quirky, more utilitarian African pots. She likes to use pure wool yarns in their natural state to echo the integrity of the classic ceramic materials of the potter.

As knitted textiles have undergone a reappraisal, so too have macramé and crochet. These traditional textile techniques use the looped stitch and knots respectively. Together with knitting they have had connotations of low-level craft activities.

However macramé meets high-tech in the marriage of handcraft and industrial technology in Dutch designer Marcel Wanders's knotted rope chair. First produced in green in 1996, and distributed by Italian furniture company Cappellini, it has recently been reissued in red in a limited edition of 99. The chair's lightness and strength comes from its macramé structure; the rope is made of an aramide braid with a carbon fibre centre that is then impregnated with epoxy resin and hung on a frame to harden. Gravity dictates its final shape.

Iconic designers concerned with textile development push the parameters of textile technology. This is particularly true of the Japanese designers, whose work is materials based, and concerned with form and structure, a result of their traditional craft skills deployed in the weaving and dyeing associated with the making of kimonos. Paradoxically, investment has made Japanese technology the most advanced in the world. One of the most

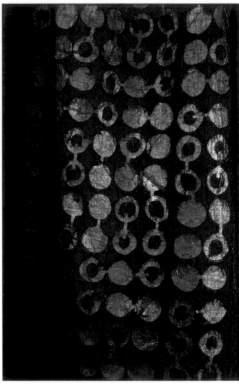

The NUNO Corporation combines traditional textile techniques with innovative industrial processes that have an impact on the textile, interior design and fashion industries worldwide.

Above. NUNO TSUNAGI: Designed by Yuka Taniguchi this is one of a series of fabrics in the Tsunagi patchwork series. Scraps of various NUNO fabrics are appliquéd by hand on to a transparent base.

Above right. HOSHIGAKI: Designer Ryoko Sugiura was inspired by the Japanese tradition of hanging up strings of persimmons to freeze dry under the thatched eaves of farmhouses. NUNO applies strings of the fruit made from Japanese handmade paper known as *washi* on to a linen base with durable synthetic glue.

Right. WINDBREAK: Cut weaving involves 'floating' loose thread structures that are then cut by hand or machine. Here, the transparency of the monofilament threads and fringes – first rough-cut by hand, then evened off with a cropping machine – are exploited in this seemingly weightless design by Tomoko Sasaki.

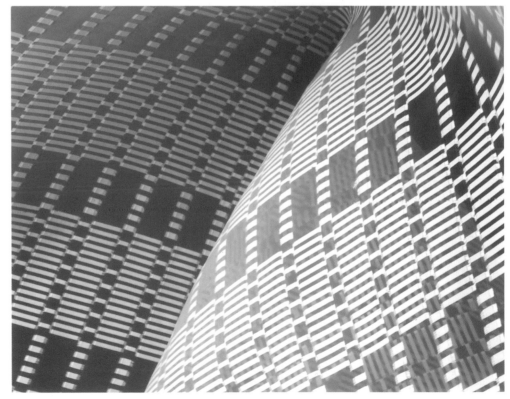

Above. RETEX OSHIMA: Designed by Reiko Sudo, one of the founders of the NUNO Corporation, using Oshima *tsumugi* from the Amami Oshima island. Left over 'waste' threads are collected, respun and used to make new thread.

Above right. TSUGIHAGI (BASHO): This 'swatchbuckle' fabric, designed by Kazuhiro Ueno and engineered by Reiko Sudo, deploys the traditional technique of devoré. The surface is comprised of remnants of various NUNO fabrics, cut into squares and sewn onto the surface. Dissolving the base fabric then leaves the patchwork of fabrics on a lacy ground.

significant figures in textile innovation, Jun'ichi Arai has for five decades combined various traditional weaving techniques with advanced textile technology, applying his ingenuity to fabrics for all of the major Japanese fashion designers such as Issey Miyake, Yohji Yamamoto and Commes des Garçons. For many years he explored the use of polyester slit-film, a type of yarn made by vacuum-sealing a layer of metal such as titanium, chrome or aluminium to a nylon/polyester base membrane, which is then slit into strips for thread. Using the innate behaviour of various yarns such as these and the thermoplastic memory of synthetic fibres, together with new interpretations of age-old techniques, the fabrics achieve museum status.

Designers continually surprise and confound the human eye and challenge traditional values of what is considered conventionally beautiful or precious. The Japanese aesthetic is enshrined in the word *wabi* for which there is no European

equivalent. It describes finding beauty in the simple and unpretentious, the subtle hues of grey, black and brown. Fashion historian Caroline Evans takes it further: 'If in traditional Japanese aesthetics *wabi sabi* attributes a superior value, based on enlightened recognition, to the flawed artefact and to poor materials, in a modern consumer economy the style of *wabi sabi* only becomes valuable when it is used to create a consumer discourse of the avant-garde.'[1]

The aesthetic of *boro boro*, meaning ragged or dilapidated, whereby fabrics are boiled, slashed, shredded or dropped in acid, was a concept initially developed by the NUNO Corporation, a global leader in experimental fashion and interior textiles, founded in 1984 by Jun'ichi Arai and Reiko Sudo. This process is far removed from the clichéd 'shabby chic' faux history of distressed paintwork and faded chintz. This is a point of view embraced in the 1990s by European 'deconstructivist'

Previous spread. Harmonious colours – those close to each other in the spectrum – and the lightness of touch created by lightweight transparent natural fibres inspire a feeling of movement in the home and fashion textiles of Jürgen Lehl.

The introduction of colour in the designer's woven textiles has a quality of painterly mark making; drawn on cloth with collage and appliqué, the broken lines have the characteristics of a brushstroke.

fashion designers such as Martin Margiela and Ann Demeulemeester, who created garments that showed the processes of their manufacture, with hanging threads and raw edges. As the fashion circle turns, and once again these designers are being reappraised, this concept can increasingly be seen in contemporary product design whereby imperfections are a device deployed by the designer to imbue the piece with the fallibility of the human hand. Hella Jongerius uses cross-stitching to hold the upholstery in place on her 'Polder' sofa for Vitra, deliberately leaving loose threads hanging. Patricia Urquiola allows strips of

bare canvas to show alongside the tufted areas in the rugs she is designing for Morosa that provide an artisanal quality to the work.

Such imperfections also attract designer Jürgen Lehl. Although born in Poland and of German nationality, he decided to stay in Japan after going there on holiday in 1971. He set up his ready-to wear clothing business in 1972 eventually adding to his practice fabrics for interiors, bed linen, furniture and jewelry. Fusing western and eastern sensibilities he is intrigued by the possibility of producing seemingly effortless variety, randomness and irregularity in spite of an industry geared to manufacture textiles that are uniform in weave and structure. 'To choose techniques that are not fully controllable, to find the weaknesses of the machine, to use repeats that are bigger than the field of vision to cheat the unsuspecting eye are some ways of breaking this tedium,'[2] he explains. These non-repeating patterns are developed in both weave and knit techniques; sometimes the cloth will go

Jacquard looms have the potential to create intricate designs and a great variety of scale. For furnishing fabrics, these large areas of pattern may be used to evoke the wall coverings of antique tapestries. The many samples on the open shelves are contemporary records of the company's output.

through several processes in different countries: woven in India, embroidered in China and finally *shibori* dyed in Japan – the ancient 'shaped resist' method of stitched and bound cloth that is then dip dyed before finally being made up into a garment.

Noble fibres

Even in periods of modernity, haute couture has signified its enduring values by an adhesion to the hierarchy of luxury materials. Certain qualities of materials and fibres have always been reserved for the highest market levels. This reverence for the luxurious is also enshrined in the iconography of couture interiors. The singular vision of the couturier is divorced from the reality of market trends. This freedom from the restraints of commerciality (couture is very often a 'loss leader' and a way of promoting a range of products such as accessories, scent and cosmetics) means that the most luxurious materials and the most labour-intensive processes

are at their disposal; feathers specially farmed in South Africa, braid for the house of Chanel painstakingly made by hand by the one remaining artisan, 75-year-old Madame Pouzieux, who works in a barn outside her farmhouse ninety minutes' drive from Paris. Each thread from a bale of cloth is unravelled by hand and the fibres woven into braid, the colours in exact proportion to the cloth, on her specially customized hand loom. An equivalent in the world of interiors is the work of the highly skilled *passementiers*, such as those at French firm Michel Sahuc, who produce luxurious decorative trimmings of tassels, fringes and braid, used to adorn furniture and furnishings.

Couturiers and high-profile interior designers are able to call upon the expertise of a range of suppliers of woven, printed and embroidered textiles who are eager to provide a personalized service, offering suggestions and swatches but who are ultimately at the disposal of the designer.

'Guard' books, an archive of each and every design produced by Stephen Walters and Sons, record all the technical information needed to replicate a design. As trends in fashion and interiors tend to be cyclical, these archives are one of the most valuable resources of textile manufacturers. Changing something as simple as the colouration of a design can render an archive textile contemporary.

Computer-driven technology enables these suppliers to do the short runs of specially commissioned dyed, woven and printed cloth required. Looms are customized to produce a particular effect, and methods fiercely guarded, lest the technique be leaked to countries that have the capacity to manufacture cheaply, but who are without the technical and design expertise necessary to initiate the process. The interiors equivalent to the couturier's atelier is the workshop of the furniture maker, where cabinet makers, inlayers, French polishers and upholsterers, highly skilled and experienced craftspeople, process rare woods and luxurious specially dyed and woven fabrics into couture products for the home.

Globalization means that fabric sourcing is no longer a local enterprise; basic production has been outsourced to those countries where labour is cheap, particularly China, and more recently India, Vietnam and Bangladesh (where labour

costs are cheaper than China). Franco Milotti, head of Milior, the European textile company in Prato, initially responsible for the innovative stretch fabrics behind Prada and the 'techno' look of the 1990s, is now developing a new range of fabrics for the top end of the market, fabrics that are limited in quantity, different and highly creative. He says of China, 'All our customers are buying from China, but they also understand that they cannot survive with Chinese goods alone. That's because the Chinese are not good at everything. If you want something fast, or a little bit crazy, you have to make it nearer to home.'[3] Home, in this case, means Europe.

The original couturiers of Paris, London and Florence (the Italian fashion venue that preceded Milan) operated within a network of specialized textile manufacturers such as the silk weavers Bianchini-Ferier in Lyons, France, and in Suffolk, England. The weaving of 'noble fibres' such as cashmere and silk has long been the prerogative

Samples are reworked by drawing on the computer, which then relays the information directly to the jacquard loom. The implementation of computer-aided design has created a greater flexibility in weaving the shorter runs required for fashion. Woven fabrics for interior purposes generally have a longer production run due to a slower turnover and greater volume. The cones of coloured silk suspended over the loom are there to effect repairs.

of Stephen Walters and Sons. Originally founded by Huguenot weavers in 1720, the company settled in London's Spitalfields before moving to Suffolk, where a declining woollen industry had already moved north in search of more powerful water supplies. This meant that there was an established and skilled workforce in place.

Julius Walters, managing director of Stephen Walters and Sons, is the ninth generation to be involved in the company's long history of silk weaving. In his office hangs a portrait of his forebear Joseph Walters, painted by Gainsborough in 1725. During the Victorian period the company wove black mourning crepe and parasol silks; parachute silk was produced during World War II; and the contemporary output is for haute couture labels such as Chanel, Giles and Prada. Producing bespoke fabrics for the fashion industry involves four collections a year. Walters explains, 'Because the company has the capacity and flexibility to do short runs,

we are able to produce thousands of designs a year. High-speed rapier looms together with electromagnetic jacquards are linked to design computers to produce maximum flexibility in the production of relatively short lengths of cloth. Everything is woven to order; we don't make to stock.'

The discriminating world of haute couture demands that the company focuses on the client's exacting requirements. 'We don't overly concern ourselves with trends,' Walters states, 'A trend may not be right for the customer. Instead we try to innovate. The balance is to create something radically new whilst still keeping true to the designer/brand identity.'

The sister company, David Walters Fabrics, specializes in textiles for interiors. 'In the twenty-first century there has been a greater awareness of the influence of fashion in interiors,' confirms Richard Searles, sales director of David Walters Fabrics, 'particularly in the use of colour. Consumers are much bolder in their

A pinboard at Stephen Walters and Sons (opposite) showing swatches of cloth that have gone on to appear on the catwalk in collections by designers, such as Giles (above right).

requirements now. Colour is what dates a design; a traditional pattern that we may have taken from the archive can look completely different and utterly contemporary by simply changing the colours.' The floor-to-ceiling shelves of the archive room contain swatches and sample books dating from the earliest days of the company, including ornate and decorative fragments of brocade (the colours unfaded) used for waistcoats made for mid-nineteenth-century gentlemen. Records of contemporary designs are referenced and cross-referenced using a detailed system to verify provenance and to provide specifications for any further production.

Fashion has also influenced the speed at which interior fabrics change. 'We used to keep a design in production for several decades, but now it's a matter of revolution, not evolution.' There remain, however, some differences. 'Unlike the fashion market we would expect a design

to be in production for three years to pay for the initial design and development of the product.' In contrast Julius Walters of the fashion company describes the search for the fresh and innovative as 'insatiable. As soon as a trend becomes apparent; you have to have a new idea. The more we can create, the more people want. If a design is well received and copied then couturiers are eager to do something completely different the following season.'

Techniques and innovations, as well as colour, cross the boundaries between the fabrics for interiors and those for fashion. As Richard Searles points out, 'Different weave constructions can translate very well from one area to another; we might change the weight of the yarn, or the scale of the pattern but the construction will be common to both.'

Just as in fashion there is the requirement for the special piece, the brocade coat or silk and cashmere jacquard woven jacket, the fashion in interiors is

Sustainable textiles by Carey Young using recycled metal, second-hand leather and regenerated wool, all dyed with natural dyestuffs that use low-energy products. The lampshades are made from recycled catering packs and recycled wire and are decorated with strips of recycled paper from magazines. Designers concerned with sustainability tend to investigate materials, processes and techniques that have an innate versatility and that can be applied to products for both fashion and interiors.

now also about the unique, bespoke piece. There is a current trend to have just one length and use it as a wall hanging, very much as the Elizabethans did with their tapestries. In the 1980s there was overwhelming use of pattern, but now the direction is for signature pieces, such as a damask, a historic weave that has a reversible pattern of satin and matt, usually deployed for large-scale florals, that can be placed in a neutral setting. Historical authenticity, forward- looking design and technical innovation enable the companies Stephen Walters and Sons and David Walters Fabrics to offer the best, both to their couture clients and to the interior fabrics market. As Julius Walters points out, 'there is an artisan element in what we do; it is very labour-intensive, even though the manufacturing processes are highly technical. More importantly, we stay in business because we develop new ideas.'

Moral fibres

The provenance of knitted, woven and embellished textiles for both fashion and interiors was once easily identified; their manufacture usually taking place in areas that have traditionally produced these specialized products. Lyons in France and Suffolk in England for silk weaving, Como in Italy for silk printing, the ateliers of Paris for embroidery, are all renowned for the longevity and traditions of their particular crafts and skills. However, the contemporary globalization of the mass market has meant that the ethically aware consumer now needs to question the source, both of the raw materials and their manufacture, of the products that they buy. This desire of some consumers for the organic and eco-friendly, as well as concern for the provenance of products and the desire to recycle and reclaim materials, is providing designers with new challenges.

Sustainability means to keep going, the very antithesis of fashionability, and

Above. Danish fashion label Noir uses organically certified African cotton and is to launch a cotton brand, Illuminati II, to supply sub-Saharan cotton to luxury brands. A percentage of profits from the clothes go to Africa to support the cotton workers. 'We want to be known as the first brand to turn corporate social responsibility sexy,' says Peter Ingwersen, founder of Noir. Their foundation provides essential medicine and micro loans in a scheme called Humane Business Model.

Above right and opposite. Edun's mission statement is 'to increase trade and create sustainable employment for developing areas of the world with an emphasis on Africa, providing a business model that others can replicate and follow.'

yet sustainable design is a concept that is currently preoccupying designers of both fashion and interiors. Author and academic Dr Tim Willey describes true sustainability as a product being perpetually in a cycle. 'Some processes sound sustainable, but merely prolong the existence of a product, momentarily pulling it out of its life-cycle. We should be looking at true sustainability rather than removing something from the loop before it ends in landfill.'

Although sustainability has become the new buzzword and is an increasingly essential element in the manufacture and marketing of products, there are fears that sustainability will become just another trend. Fashion is principally about image, rather than survival, and simply having attractive products does not necessarily provide enough impetus for people to make real changes. Indeed, only threats to the ecosystem will do that. An analogy can be drawn with the use of fur in fashion and interiors. There was a time when the decision whether

or not to use and wear fur had a moral basis, yet it is now used unapologetically, almost defiantly. The movement towards sustainability may be just as ephemeral.

The difficulty has always been to reconcile the affordable and sustainable with the aesthetically pleasing. It is not enough that products are simply worthy exercises in restraint, or that they exist because it is expedient to be politically correct in marketing the brand. There are of course other consumers who welcome the arrival of the £10 dress or the £2 cushion, and have no concern for its real costs in terms of sweated labour or the fact that cotton is one of the world's most destructive crops, often processed in near-slavery conditions.

For those who are concerned with the provenance of their clothes British designer Katharine Hamnett has been at the forefront of fashion accountability with her ranges of organic cotton since the 1980s, and her desire, now, is for everyone to buy at least one organic cotton item a year. London

Fashion Week in 2006 saw her first 100% ethical clothing range, the same year that the British Fashion Council initiated its 'estethica division' – retail space devoted to designers with an ethical stance. Peter Ingwersen, a Dane, and one half of the design label Noir, offers a demi-couture approach. 'I totally respect what everyone is doing for ethical clothing, but at the same time I don't want to be lumped as "that ethical clothes label". Our garments look like normal stylish clothes made from luxurious fabrics and unless you knew about us, you'd never guess the organic provenance.'[4]

Textile designer Jürgen Lehl eschews the use of synthetic materials entirely. 'When reading about the very polluting production and disposal of polyester in a trade journal 25 years ago, I decided to only use natural materials.' His design philosophy is equally rigorous. 'When I was a child my mother told me not to litter, to keep things around me in order and clean. This simple teaching is what rules my choices in design to this

day. I use materials that can be returned to the soil without problems. I design things that are useful, simple and practical. The most important design decision is whether what I want to do next is necessary or not.'

The label Edun, brainchild of U2 frontman Bono and his wife Ali Hewson, together with New York clothing designer Rogan Gregory, is bringing sophisticated design to fair-trade clothes. Under the banner of (PRODUCT)[RED], The Gap, Motorola, American Express, Converse and Armani have all committed a percentage of their profits on RED products to the Global Fund to fight HIV/Aids, TB and malaria in Africa for five years, including the profits of an edition of Britain's *Independent* newspaper guest-edited by Giorgio Armani. These global brands do not differentiate in quality of design between their other products and those under the RED label. Trainers designed by Giles Deacon and made up in African printed mud cloth for Converse are desirable in themselves, not

Haute couture by Deborah Milner takes sustainability and accountability to a high aesthetic level with base materials transformed into luxury. The dress is constructed from recycled plastic lace using the Japanese *shibori* technique. After tying small knots from white plastic bags, pieces were hot ironed between tracing paper, melting the plastic into 'lace', which was then mounted onto silk tulle and appliquéd with Swarovski crystals. The 'Rousseau' dress (overleaf), inspired by the layering of leaf shapes in the Brazilian rain forest, was created with fabric donated by Mantero Seta from an old stock of tie fabrics, and hand sewn using a mixture of appliqué and reverse appliqué.

just because they sustain the economy of a small village in Africa. In collaboration with Gap, French designer Roland Mouret has produced a collection of ten dresses, with half the profits going to the Global Fund. Scarlett Johansson is the face of RED for Emporio Armani, lending an inevitable celebrity cachet to the cause.

The consumer will always be seduced by the look of something and what it will add to their life in terms of enjoyment, pleasure and status. We fall in love with a product, and it takes someone of great determination and strength of will to defer gratification of this sort for the rights of an unknown worker in a far-off country, or to be concerned with the process of slaughtering animals for their skins when the result is literally a pair of shoes 'to die for'. Designers such as Stella McCartney have the stout-heartedness and the moral scruples to refuse to use materials such as leather, but consumers love her shoes because of the design, and would buy them anyway, leather or plastic.

It is particularly demanding to create couture from sources that are sustainable; natural products are of fluctuating quality and indeterminate longevity. As British designer Deborah Milner explains, 'It is difficult to find couture-quality sustainable textiles and dyes; most do not meet the exacting standards required for high fashion design.' A successful couturier, Milner took leave of absence to live and work in Brazil, a move that inspired her to combine her couture expertise with research into sustainability, aided by globally recognized plant-based cosmetic brand Aveda. Founded by environmentalist Horst M. Rechelbacher in 1978, the company funded research into an ecologically sound range of couture dresses; the result is the Aveda 'Ecoture'™ collection. Each dress specifically seeks solutions to an environmental problem, and sources responsibly harvested materials such as hand-woven silk by a fair trade collective in India, 'Women Weave'. The recycled white plastic bags of the

Hussein Chalayan's 'After Words' collection explores the concept of portable architecture, and was inspired by the necessity for people displaced by war and invasion to carry their homes when fleeing a country and becoming nomadic. The table and chairs were constructed by Scottish maker and product designer Paul Topen.

bridal lace dress are far removed from traditional couture materials but produce a convincing facsimile of lace once heat pressed, mounted on tulle and appliquéd.

One of the world's leading silk distribution and production companies, Mantero Seta, sited in Como, northern Italy, is also cooperating on the project. Aiming to have 'zero environmental impact' on the planet, the company made a silk faille, a ribbed lightweight silk, for Milner, which was yarn dyed with natural dyes, difficult to do to a couture standard if it were not undertaken by a company used to creating couture fabrics. Mantero also donated some of the fabrics for the project from their stock of surplus silk and this recycled tie stock of jacquards and brocades has also gone into the 'Rousseau' dress, inspired by the designer's trips to the rainforest. It took textile designer Karen Spurgin four months to embroider the dress with a complex technique of appliqué and reverse appliqué. The Mantero design studio is

currently researching fibres, dyes and fabric structures towards creating fabrics for haute couture with environmental integrity, and has developed 'Resilk', a new felt product composed of 50% superfluous silk and 50% wool fibres.

Sourcing the sustainable

In interiors this concern for the environment is reflected in the growing desire for a 'green' lifestyle, particularly as buildings are increasingly required by law to fulfil certain ecologically sound criteria, using sustainable materials and saving energy. Concern for the world's finite resources is reflected in the choices made by the ethically responsible consumer: natural paints based on oils, simple minerals and plant products rather than polluting solvents; floors of stone or wood rather than vinyl, which is made from polyvinyl chloride that leaks hormone disrupting phthalates into the environment; hemp, with its greater yields per acre, rather than cotton; and wool, which author and

Left. French design house Roche-Bobois
has an eco-friendly collection designed by
Christophe Delcourt that uses sustainable
Bourguignon forest wood and is assembled
without the use of glue or stains.

Opposite. The corrugated cardboard and metal
sofa by Fernando and Humberto Campana was
inspired by the cardboard collected each day
for recycling by the poor of São Paulo in Brazil.

academic Dr Willey describes as 'basically
sunlight', a locally sourced product that is
'incredibly sustainable'. Concern about the
possible carcinogenic compounds and other
toxic materials used in the manufacturing
and finishing of many products means that
for many consumers choice is to do with the
integrity of the product, and not the design.

Dutch designer Marcel Wanders takes
a pragmatic approach. 'I'm not the kind
of guy to work on lil' inventions to save
the world. I work with durability in
design, products worth bonding with for
a lifetime…in the face of a throwaway
culture that consumes meaningless
products, I want my creations to have
more quality…I'm a sort of amateur;
amateurs aren't so sure about things so

they investigate and sometimes find an
interesting solution, bringing new ideas to
it that experts might overlook. I have an
overall respect for us and the world – and
I think that is the basis of "good design".'[5]

Recycling in creative ways is now also
the preoccupation of the avant-garde, with
designers who function at the top end of
the market producing one-off pieces whose
price reflects the purity of their process
and source. French furniture designer
Christophe Delcourt uses locally sourced
oak (for each tree that is felled, another is
planted) that is sawn in mills that recycle
the sawdust. His designs for Roche-Bobois
include a tree-like bookcase, artisan in
appearance in a way that conveys the ethos
behind it. Sustainable design does not

Architects Nick Eldridge and Piers Smerin designed 'Anyroom;Everyroom', in conjunction with joinery specialists Opus Magnum, to challenge the conventional use of living space within contemporary environments. The honeycomb-like birch-ply structure can be assembled within an existing room or space, and the integral furnishings are made from sustainable materials, such as wool and rubber. Incorporated into the design is pull-out felt-topped seating, a suspended felt magazine rack, a television platform and a writing desk.

Opposite. This recycled cardboard chintz chair by Factum, overlaid with an intricate print, overcomes assumptions about flat-pack furniture. Easy to use, as well as being aesthetically exciting, it unfolds in seconds. Cardboard furniture is lightweight, affordable and easily transportable. Once it has reached the end of its life, it can be recycled again.

Above. The 'Tide' chandelier by Stuart Haygarth shows the many types and colours of transparent glass that can be sourced from a single stretch of beach on the Kent coast of England.

have to be literal, of course. It is also an opportunity for designers to be playful, and surprise us with unexpected materials.

Designer Tony Davis of Art Meets Matter believes that sustainability is not the prerogative of the precious. He launched the Factum range of designs at 100% Design with the cardboard 'Chintz' chair that subverts the notion of traditionally patterned furniture with a low-tech approach to problem solving. 'I had a specific reason for designing the chair, a child of six could put it together, there are no instructions, and it is not embarrassed about being decorative. The surface, designed by Angela Lambert, says precious and decorative and expensive, but you can hang it on the wall or post it to anywhere in the world. The chair is the beginnings of a range that explores the use of simple recycled

materials but doesn't ignore people's desire for decoration and surface pattern.'

Combining the roles of eco-warrior and cardboard engineer, Davis declares his intention of providing products created from individual materials that are already nearly 100% recyclable and have a usable life. 'We say "use it, don't lose it", I think a lot of worthy recycling is actually making use of third-world labour and cheap materials, which are then shipped halfway around the world before they reach the customer. When you make things for sale you have by necessity to make choices about quality. Objects that may still be functional but have some visual flaws are being junked by every company you can name.' Davis also feels that traditional retailing practices are responsible for the inaccessibility of good design. 'Designers sometimes strip away humanity, they do not allow imperfections, but why not have idiosyncrasy and variety? Someone like Frank Gehry makes a one-off sofa that costs thousands of dollars and it appears in one shop window, but I think exclusivity is inappropriate, and certainly not the future. Things will be exclusive not because they cost a lot of money, but because they are personal to the individual. We now customize our environment.'

The customization of clothes has always been a popular activity in fashion. The perennial appeal of vintage clothing and the cyclical nature of fashion are also reflected in the desire to appropriate elements of the past and the used into contemporary interiors. The recycling of clothes, fabrics and furniture certainly extends the life-cycle of these products, and fuels many creative initiatives, from furniture found in skips and reupholstered, to chandeliers made from beach detritus, such as the 'Tide' chandelier by Stuart Haygarth.

It is irrefutable that sustainability should be inherent in the design process, and that no design can be considered 'good' unless it goes some way to address issues of social context and the impact of the product on the environment. Fortunately, as contemporary designers are now addressing issues of ethical trading and enthusiastically exercising restraint in terms of sustainability, it is no longer a matter of the consumer having to choose between aesthetics and the environmentally friendly. Being ecologically aware is no longer perceived as risible; a movement that began with concern over the safety and sustainability of food has now extended into all aspects of life, from fashion to interiors and from transport to architecture.

Handmade details restore authenticity in these natural forms by Jürgen Lehl, which are the antithesis of high tech.

Chapter four Liaisons

Accessories are essential to the financial success of a label. Extending their signature style into products for the home, exclusive fashion companies such as Versace, Hermès, Missoni and Roberto Cavalli allow the customer to buy into the brand in much the same way that cosmetics and beauty products commercially uphold a couture fashion label. This diversification is facilitated by the globalization of manufacturing processes and provides widespread recognition of the signature style of the brand in a way that aims to sustain rather than undermine its design integrity. The demand for luxury means that for those unable to afford an Armani evening dress, there is always the opportunity to buy an Armani/Casa cushion that might placate the desire for the new and the covetable, just as the lipstick or the scent is an affordable way to buy into the glamour of the Dior or Chanel label.

Fashion has now permeated global twenty-first-century culture in a way unprecedented in previous times. The demand for designed goods is universal, inevitably leading to mass production. Retailers have identified the crossover between 'mass' and 'prestige' as 'masstige', the point where iconic designers are commissioned to produce an affordable diffusion line for the mass market, or a global brand offers low-price articles to enable everyone to access the label. Fashion-related products – the 'add-ons' – contribute significantly to the label in financial terms. Even when the global economy is in recession and the market difficult, the luxury business continues to grow, and the desire for accessories appears to be unlimited. In this way products for interiors achieve 'must have' status on a par with the iconic dress or bag in fashion. Journalist Bryan Appleyard describes 'must have' as 'a brilliant phrase that sums up the peculiar will to subjugation involved in the pursuit of fashion'.[2] It describes the desire of the consumer to participate

'I want to make things that girls will love more than their handbags.'
Marcel Wanders[1]

Print design 'Peggy' on a lamp base by Spanish fashion label Ailanto for Spanish ceramic company Sargadelos.

During the mid-1960s French couturier Pierre Cardin embraced space-age technology in his hard-edged futuristic fashion designs, such as this pinafore dress from 1969. The same preoccupation with futuristic shapes and reflective surfaces can be seen in his collaboration with architect Antti Lovag, in the house Le Palais Bulles, in Théoule-sur-Mer on the French Riviera.

in all aspects of lifestyle marketing.

The impetus for fashion designers to move into interiors and products for the home is a relatively modern phenomenon. Parisian couturiers, beginning with Elsa Schiaparelli in 1935, sold ready-made fashion accessories in a 'boutique' appended to the couture salon, but Pierre Cardin was the first couturier to apply a brand licensing system in 1960, extending the parameters of his practice to cover all aspects of lifestyle living. However licensing is a commercial process whereby the designer allows their name to be used without them necessarily being involved in either the design or the manufacturing process. This can sometimes result in the brand being devalued.

Mark Eley of Eley Kishimoto believes that the nature of the connection between fashion and interiors has to some extent been rendered superficial because of this. 'Over the past 30 years barriers have been breaking down, and design now has very few boundaries. This is not a bad thing if

the company has creatively good intentions. Sub-licensing and secondary designs that involve sending a mood board to a company who then come up with a product to market commercially have a detrimental result on design.' In contrast Eley Kishimoto prefer the collaborative approach. 'We continue to act with the same ethos that we have always done, and as we did with the original company. We don't instigate, we participate,' says Eley. Projects include sportswear, luggage and furniture. 'Creative precedents have been truly pushed on an independent level. Our collaborations are the result of our relationships, we approach design with a different drive; integrity, experimentation and warmth. We have a portfolio of intimacy.'

Legendary Italian fashion label Pucci was one of the first fashion labels to make a foray into the homeware market in 1972. Among the foremost print designers of the twentieth century, Marchese Emilio Pucci di Barsento produced dazzling prints on

London design duo Mark Eley and Wakako Kishimoto's unique design sensibility includes fashion, product design, furniture, luggage, wallpapers and ceramics and furnishing fabrics. The label's iconic 'Flash' design, based on animal prints, and with a repeat pattern of only twenty square centimetres was their first design to travel across products and seasons.

The fluid psychedelic patterning of Italian label Pucci's signature prints animates the sofa by Patrick Norguet from the 'Rive Droite' range, upholstered in one of Pucci's archive prints, and is also evident in the dress by Pucci for Spring/Summer 2007.

stretch fabrics that captured the mood of the jet-setting 1960s, and a new era of relaxed, informal dressing that combined athleticism with modernity, clothes that were enjoyed by Marilyn Monroe and Jackie Kennedy. An entrepreneur, as well as designer and inventor, Pucci licensed his fabrics to upholstery and accessory firms; one of his most successful furnishing textiles was the 1963 'Fantasiosa' print. The vibrant psychedelic swirls of colour of the print maestro attracted the eye of Argentinean rug producer Dandolo y Primi and a range of rugs was launched at the Museum of Decorative Arts in Buenos Aires in 1972. These remain a significant aspect of the Pucci homeware collection, which now includes French designer Patrick Norguet's 'Rive Droite' range, and Piero Lissoni's 'Swimming Pool' collection, made up of fifteen seats of different sizes, and available in three archive Pucci prints. Rather than manufacturing products in-house both furniture ranges

are manufactured and distributed in conjunction with Italian furniture company Cappellini. Pucci's daughter, Laudomia Pucci, continued to design after her father's death in 1992 and continues as image director. The label was taken over by the French luxury conglomerate LVMH (Moët Hennessy – Louis Vuitton) in 2000 and Pucci is now fronted by British designer Matthew Williamson, who is no stranger to extending his personal aesthetic across the boundaries of fashion and interiors.

Liaisons between manufacturing companies and designers may involve companies with a 'heritage' who wish to connect to a contemporary aesthetic, such as Spanish ceramic company Lladro's new collection with Bodo Sperlein, Irish company Waterford Crystal with John Rocha, or British company Wedgwood with Jasper Conran. Liaisons, however, also provide the impetus for the forming of a new business, as is the case with Spanish company DAC, now commissioning

The austere classicism of Jasper Conran's menswear is mirrored in the neo-classical decoration of British china company Wedgwood's Jasper Ware, which has remained a constant of their product range since 1775. However, the Jasper Conran 'Chinoiserie' collection for Wedgwood is a sumptuous fusion of traditional adornment and contemporary vitality.

Spain's foremost fashion designers such as Jordi Labanda and Christian Hoyos to design rugs and carpets.

Jasper Conran is one of the most successful independent designers in Britain with an annual turnover of £250 million. He has long acknowledged the confluence of trends in fashion and interiors. 'I've always seen the connection, so in my opinion thank goodness other people are beginning to take notice. I definitely think that the whole interiors scene is becoming more and more like the fashion world. With the advent of more affordable home interior retail outlets, trends can come and go as quickly as they do in fashion. Why not?' Group communications executive at Wedgwood, Andrew Stanistreet, says that ceramics have been subject to fashion trends since the inauguration of the company in 1759. 'The original Jasper stoneware was developed out of the eighteenth-century custom of sending young aristocrats off on a Grand Tour to study European culture

and the artefacts of antiquity. They brought home with them the desire to replicate what they had seen abroad, and the founder, Josiah Wedgwood, gave it to them.'

Josiah Wedgwood and his artist John Flaxman elevated the craft of pottery into a thriving industrial business, and in doing so influenced popular taste. There are over two centuries of pattern books in the Wedgwood archive. Stanistreet says, 'Designers will look over the archives and reinterpret them, as British ceramic artist Robert Dawson has done with the willow pattern design. We never expect designers to compromise; there would be no point in asking a designer to do something and then watering it down. We take the design up to their level, often developing new glazes and colours. Non-ceramic designers bring a fresh view and are aware of current trends. They all have a proven expertise in a different field.' As Jasper Conran explains, 'My training was quite traditional in that it focused on the fundamentals of design.

Right. The inaugural collection of crystal stemware and fine bone china by influential American designer Marc Jacobs. Named after his closest friends, 'Elizabeth' (top row) and 'Jean' (bottom row), the pieces reflect the designer's contemporary interpretation of traditional elegance.

Opposite. Traditional items of homeware are constantly being updated by manufacturers to appeal to a younger, more contemporary customer. Jasper Conran's design for Waterford Crystal is 'contemporary elegance grounded in tradition'.

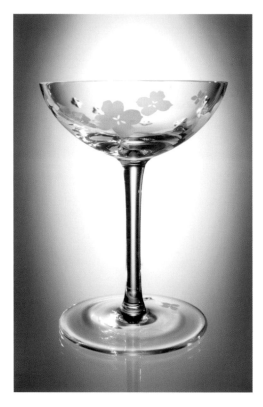

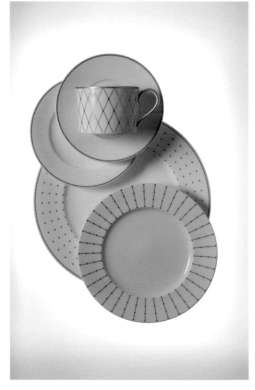

The more I worked as a designer, the more I realized those fundamentals were pretty consistent across disciplines. Just because I was doing fashion design doesn't mean I couldn't have an opinion on homeware, or furniture or interiors. Today I get to work across these disciplines and I love it.'

Changing fashions in dining also affects the tableware ranges, according to Andrew Stanistreet. 'Twenty years ago a dining service would reflect the way we ate then, organized around the standard meal of three courses with meat and vegetables. We live in a much more global society now, and the company recognizes that there are different needs today, and make tableware specifically for global cuisine such as rice and pasta.'

The reintroduction of colourways such as turquoise and taupe into Wedgwood's traditional two-coloured Jasper ware is a direct result of the contemporary desire for colour and decoration in the home. Jasper Conran explains, 'I think people

Matthew Williamson's keynote style of ebullient colour and large-scale patterning translates from catwalk to interiors, as seen in the 'Tribe' rug (opposite), designed for The Rug Company, and in the dress from his Spring/Summer 2006 collection (above). (Photograph of rug courtesy of The Rug Company.) The signature coloured stripes of British designer Paul Smith have been converted into a rhythmic pattern for the 'Swirl' rug designed for The Rug Company (above right). (Photograph courtesy of The Rug Company.)

got tired of minimal spaces that looked like empty galleries. I think they began to crave a bit of richness in their lives, which leads to pattern, texture, colour. I'm all for it – within reason of course.'

From runway to rugs

Companies such as The Rug Company frequently commission fashion designers, including the likes of Megan Park and Matthew Williamson, to produce one-off pieces, giving the designers the opportunity to rework images from the archive, changing texture, surface, scale and meaning. British designer Vivienne Westwood's 'Squiggle' rug featured a print design that first appeared in her debut catwalk collection in 1981. 'When The Rug Company approached me I knew I had all these wonderful prints that could be exploited, although obviously we have played around with the scale. It's really good to be able to translate your ideas into something else.'[3] Christopher and Suzanne Sharp set up The Rug Company in 1997,

a period when the market for traditional rugs was declining, but when there was also a trend for polished wooden floors and large loft-like spaces that necessitated an infill of colour and texture. 'The rug business is reflective, always looking back. When we started the company it was all expensive antiques or copies of antiques that your parents had bought in the 1970s and no one wants what their parents had. It was clear to us that there was a market for contemporary design.'

An introduction to Consuelo Castiglione of fashion label Marni by *Vogue*'s fashion director Lucinda Chambers was the first step. Christopher Sharp explains, 'If you want a floral patterned rug, you go to the best floral pattern designer there is.' Constructed by Tibetan weavers based in Nepal, each rug is spun, cleaned, dyed and knotted entirely by hand in ethically sound conditions taking at least four months to complete. 'The company is concerned with two things – manufacturing and establishing

Rugs are traditionally hand-woven from hand-
dyed and hand-spun wool. This method, combined
with design creativity, makes The Rug Company's
designs by Vivienne Westwood future classics.
(Photographs courtesy of The Rug Company.)

The iconic Diane von Furstenberg wrap dress first appeared in 1973, and has undergone a twenty-first-century revival in popularity. The simple structure of the dress requires a strong emphasis on colour and print, and the designer's love of surface pattern can be seen here in her two designs for The Rug Company. (Photographs of rugs courtesy of The Rug Company.)

a well-made product and applying contemporary design to these traditional techniques. In the rug business there is a big temptation to do things quickly and cheaply with a latex base and a tufting gun, but we wanted the weavers to weave the rugs in exactly the same way that their parents had done. No short cuts, it is a lovely combination.' One that is welcomed by the fashion designers invited to collaborate with the company. 'The designers contribute something we don't have, and it is a change for them to work with something that has the longevity of a rug. Rugs are indestructible, and they like doing something more permanent. Fashion moves quickly but rugs last, interior trends don't change as ferociously as with fashion.' Applying contemporary design to artisanal techniques creates future classics, Christopher Sharp believes. 'Consumers like to date items; the striped Paul Smith rug will become iconic in a few years, and will be identified as a collector's item.'

Fashion designers interested in strong colour and patterns have to address the compromises inherent in dressing the human form. The liberation of working within the rectangular 'canvas' of rugs and carpets provides them with the opportunity to experiment with bold blocks of geometric colour, here evidenced by Spanish design company Ailanto.

Some of Spain's foremost artists, illustrators and fashion designers are collaborating with Catalan rug company DAC owned by Ignacio Curt and Alfredo Muinos. Selling modern rugs in their store, BSB Alfombras, in central Barcelona, the partners became aware of a burgeoning demand for avant-garde rug design, and established the company to produce rugs designed exclusively for them by contemporary practitioners. 'All the designers selected have a background linked to the world of fashion, but we decided to contact only those creators we knew had a visual presence and the sort of strong personality that would translate into carpets.'[4] Collaborators include Jordi Labanda, David Delfin, Francesc Pons and Ailanto, the brand created by twin brothers Iñaki and Aitor Muñoz.

Based in Barcelona since 1992, Ailanto shows at both Gaudi Barcelona's Fashion Week and Cibeles Fashion Salon and sells to an international market, including Japan and the USA. The polychromatic rugs reflect an intense preoccupation with colour and form, inspired by the work of Piet Mondrian and Ellsworth Kelly. Iñaki Muñoz, who previously studied architecture, found the transition from three dimensions to two dimensions easy. 'When I am working on a garment I am not so worried about adding volume, I consider fashion design more to do with art or painting.' The label has also been commissioned to exhibit at the Textile and Architecture exhibition organized by the Institute of Architects of Catalonia (COAC), a body that defends quality Catalonian architecture, aims to preserve its historical legacy and ensures professional practice. The exhibition is to demonstrate the cross-fertilization of skills between architects and fashion and textile designers, and includes lighting designed by the label.

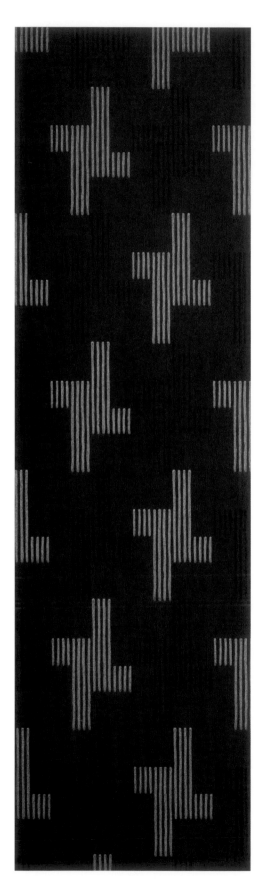

Fashion on a roll

The proliferation and popularity of bold prints, pattern and colour in fashion has now extended onto walls. After decades of neutral colours and textured surfaces in keeping with the restrained palette of minimalism, walls have ceased to be a backdrop and have become a feature in themselves. When British fashion designer Matthew Williamson was developing the design of his flagship store on London's Bruton Street he eschewed the standard boutique interior of white walls and floor in favour of a hand-blocked wallpaper designed and painted by English company de Gournay, who specialize in chinoiserie, embellishing the surface with jewels. Williamson and French couturier Roland Mouret are engaged in designing wallpapers for British company Habitat.

'People have very fixed ideas when it comes to their homes,' Williamson asserts. 'It can be very liberating to approach shopping for the house with a similar mindset to the way you buy clothes – not

throwaway, but less hidebound. Nothing has to be forever. Obviously you want to get the fundamentals right: the building itself, the furniture. But why can't you reupholster every two years? And why, if its purposes are more decorative than functional, can't it be a dress fabric?…I don't see my taste as brave. To me, painting your walls beige is a huge statement of mundanity.'[5]

Not only is a change of wallpaper one of the quickest ways to change the look of an interior, but it also provides a focus that describes the overall mood of a room and dictates the style of the furniture and artefacts. In accenting one wall, the wallpaper becomes the equivalent of a whole-wall painting. The recent revival in wallpaper was almost inevitable given the current popularity of mid-century style, a period when print and pattern were at their apotheosis.

Spearheaded by manufacturers using traditional wallpaper-making techniques, companies such as Cole & Son are retrieving

Once an anathema in the minimalist interior, wallpaper now represents the twenty-first-century desire for eclecticism, providing colour, pattern and texture. Wallpaper designs, from opposite left, are by Roland Mouret, Orla Kiely and Matthew Williamson, all in collaboration with British retailer Habitat.

designs from their archives and offering them up to the contemporary market. Cole & Son has 4,000 blocks in its archives, the earliest dating back to 1760. Other companies are following suit. Australian-born Florence Broadhurst established her wallpaper studio in the 1950s. Today, twenty years after her death, Sydney-based Signature Prints is reviving her original designs. The 1970s brightly coloured graphic and geometric designs of legendary master of pattern, British interior designer David Hicks, are being reissued by his son Ashley.

Wallpaper is not simply printing a pattern onto paper; it can be as complex as printing fabric, and many different looks can be created with the same design by the decisions made about pigments and the sequence of processes. As for many practitioners, it is the challenge of new techniques that fuels the impetus to design a new range of products. The use of gilded surfaces in design is a case in point. Wallpaper and textile designer Neisha

Wallpaper designed by Barbara Hulanicki in the spirit of Biba, the groundbreaking London store. One of the first designers to implement the concept of lifestyle marketing, iconoclastic retailer Barbara Hulanicki opened her fourth and final Biba store in 1973. The lavish art deco surroundings offered everything from homeware and foodstuffs to furniture and fashion.

A vintage chair has been upholstered in the saturated colour of print maestros Basso & Brooke's 'Cost of Beauty' collection. The plate is from the same collection, while the dramatic printed cloak is from the Spring/Summer 2007 range. In addition to its fashion collections, the label offers a bespoke service in collaboration with private clients, which includes commissions for crockery, carpets, wallpaper, tiles and glassware.

Crosland explains, 'The new metallic wallpapers come in as aluminium, and we print a tint of gold or bronze on top – but you can't tell what effect it will have on the foil until you have done it. For example, foil doesn't soak up the dye, so you get an unexpected mottled effect. You have to be there in the factory with the technician – that's why I would never have the printing done in China.' It is an expensive and time-consuming process. 'It takes about a year to produce new wallpaper, and each colour of each design needs a separate roller – these cost about £800 each. Then the dye colours in the printing process have to match my initial gouache paint colours, and I work out the colourways, which all have to work as a family. Finally, the paper is cut into 10m lengths, where accuracy is vital to the final finish – even a millimetre out and the pattern won't match once it's on the wall.'

Brazilian-born Bruno Basso and Englishman Christopher Brooke of the label Basso & Brooke first used Swarovski crystals on a dress in their 'Garden of Earthly Delights' runway collection of 2005. The luxury jewelry firm Swarovski, based in Austria, is an eager collaborator with contemporary designers, and the precision-cut crystal glass appears on both products for the home and in fashion. Brooke enjoyed the relationship. 'We talked about the initial idea for the chandelier with Swarovski, and they then researched the technique for the laser etching of the crystals. They are a great company to work for because they love the challenge of producing new processes.' Basso & Brooke are inspired colourists, renowned for their all-over engineered prints that subvert the myths and archetypes of history, mediated through a mixture of influences from Alphonse Mucha to surrealism. The prints are now being applied to products for the home. 'We usually develop the homeware range at the same time as the womenswear collection, so the buyer can develop a small story.'

Chair chic

Unlike the diversification into accessories, which is a simple extension of a product range incorporating the designer's signature style, some fashion designers enter a relationship with another practitioner that is both collaborative in concept and mutually inspirational. Japanese fashion designer Issey Miyake has always been at the forefront of technical innovation. In 1999 together with design engineer Dai Fujiwara he developed a range of avant-garde clothing called A-POC, A Piece of Cloth, a technique by which fabric, texture and either a fully finished knitted garment or the components for a fully finished woven garment are created in a single process. Such an innovative process, which has become increasingly complex as the fabric has undergone further development, is inevitably not limited to the fashion arena, and furniture maker and architect Ron Arad saw its potential. 'I thought the A-POC was a very exciting way to make garments and fabrics that are so

individual and amazingly adaptable by the end user. The idea is in contrast with the computer-controlled, industrial-machine process of making them…I thought, why can't we harness A-POC's knowledge and inventiveness in our field as well?'[6]

Already on the market was Arad's curvaceous moulded 'Ripple' chair made from a single process technique for Italian furniture manufacturer Moroso. With the introduction of the A-POC 'Gemini' chair cover, the consumer has an item that can be sat upon or worn, as the cover transforms into a sleeveless gilet. 'Borders are disappearing between disciplines, and designers should not think about them.' Fujiwara explains, 'We knew nothing about the interior world. The fashion world is about how to sell more to the consumer. That is the basic point of this collaboration. We at the Miyake design studio are used to the pace of the fashion industry and we can move faster than the interior world. The interior industry's customer buys fewer items. They use

The chair seat transforms into a duvet-style gilet in this collaboration between architect and furniture maker Ron Arad and fashion and textile designer Issey Miyake.

Paul Smith works with American company Maharam who specialize in upholstery fabrics for interior designers. 'They asked me to design for them several years ago and I have developed six designs for them so far, all based around my well-known stripes. One of the greatest difficulties has been obtaining the colour of yarns we want because the fabric has to be incredibly hard wearing and strong.'

the products they buy more, and keep them in use for longer. But sometimes they get bored. Changing the outfit can keep the chair interesting for longer.'[7]

Marcel Wanders has taken the idea of interchangeable covers one step further by offering several choices of upholstery to fit a basic 'Naked' sofa, so that changing the look of a room is as simple as changing the accessories to an outfit – upholstery as handbag. Wanders is product designer and art director of pioneering design company Moooi, a name that requisitions the Dutch word for 'beautiful' (but with an extra o for 'extra beautiful'), a company whose aim is to explore the zone between individuality and mass production.

The furniture of Paul Smith is more to do with visual puns than innovative structures, a way for the designer to reconcile the diffidence he felt about entering the furniture market. 'When I was asked by the Italian manufacturer Cappellini to design furniture for them I said no many times, and it was only after about two years of their persistence that I agreed. The reason I was reluctant was because a lot of my friends are furniture designers who are trained and skilled at this. I felt that I did not want to enter their territory. Then I decided that if I approached designing furniture in the same way as designing clothes, it may be OK. So I started with simple furniture and playing with my usual ingredient, which is surprise. For instance, a simple white chest of drawers could have a hot pink interior, or the same set of drawers could have a life-size photograph of a baroque piece of furniture making you look twice to wonder if the piece is baroque or modern.'

Collaboration is a two-way process; manufacturers are imbued with the glamour and added value of association with the design sensitivities of the fashion world, and a designer may partner a manufacturing company to enhance their design profile and extend their activities into areas not normally accessible to them. The result is a proliferation of products that sustain and fulfil the contemporary desire for the designed object.

Fendi Casa uses the same materials and high standards of manufacture as its fashion brand: furs and leathers, Swarovski drops, printed silks, fringes and studs. The famous hand-stitching, 'Selleria', used on Fendi bags, also appears on Fendi Casa's sofa and cushions.

Fendi Casa reflects the same preoccupation with luxury leathers and furs as the fashion label Fendi. This Italian fashion brand is led by creative director Karl Lagerfeld who is responsible for creating the inverted FF logo. Giovanna Golmelli at Fendi explains, 'Fendi Casa is linked to the same philosophy and directed towards the same concepts as the fashion brand. This is the reason that Fendi Casa has developed the finishes, the details, the colours and the precious materials.'

Designers are increasingly compelled to offer a total look, rooted in a visible and established brand identity where fashion and interiors are fused into a signature style. Fashion labels such as Giorgio Armani, Donna Karan and Calvin Klein recognize that customers require more than clothes from a brand, that there is a potential market for home interiors that reflect the visual identity of the label. Lifestyle products such as bedding, furniture, paint and fabrics bring the skills of the professional designer into the realms of home and domesticity for those consumers who are happy to let the brand take over the decision-making process in putting together an interior look.

Ralph Lauren was the first company to make substantial capital out of the desire of the consumer to extend their identification with a particular label beyond the boundaries of fashion. The success of the label is predicated on fulfilling all the needs of the customer from underwear and bath oil to an evening dress worthy of the Hollywood red carpet. Lauren launched his home range in 1983, and has one of the few homeware collections that can stand independently of its fashion connection and addresses comprehensively all aspects of the designed interior. Appropriating the signature style of a big brand is a fail-safe way of reassuring those who feel they lack the discernment necessary to make their own choices by borrowing a lifestyle that most closely approximates their aspirations.

French-born Nicole Farhi opened her flagship store for lifestyle products in 1994 on London's New Bond Street. This European paean to simplicity and sensual textures was followed by the US flagship store sited off Madison Avenue in New York, and both include a restaurant, Nicole's, beneath the store. The unstructured shapes and natural hues of the clothes are reflected in the use of materials in the homeware range, launched in 1998. Marble, slate, silk and blown glass from Tunisia are used

'Roll me in designer sheets.'

'Call me', Blondie, 1980

Simple, organic shapes, where the materials and processes used dictate the design of the object, exemplify the aesthetic of Nicole Farhi, which is also reflected in her fashion: simple shapes in tactile fabrics in a range of neutral colours.

Polychromatic warp-knitted stripes were for many years the unmistakable signature of Italian company Missoni, evidence of Rosita and Tai Missoni's virtuosity with the knitting machine. This confident assertion of pattern and colour is now translated by different techniques and materials into products for the home.

for tableware, ceramics and accessories. The designer explains, 'the emphasis is ultimately on tactile fabrics and a desire for absolute comfort. It is a quiet collection that is confident and clean, eschewing colour to explore variations of grey.' Both collections for the home and the catwalk grow organically, rather than seasonally changing, 'What I like about it is that it's friendly, it's not smart, and it has comfortable, warm appeal.'

In contrast, Rosita Missoni, creative director of Missoni Home, claims not to be a product designer, 'I simply apply patterns to things.' Missoni Home is an offshoot of the iconic Italian label Missoni, renowned for their polychromatic patterned knitwear

and at the forefront of the contemporary fashion into interiors phenomenon. Founded by Rosita and Tai Missoni in 1953, the label underwent a radical refocusing in 2001 when Rosita Missoni handed over the creative directorship of the company to her daughter, preferring to concentrate her creative energies on the homeware range. 'Ten years ago when Angela, our daughter, decided she was ready to take over the torch of the women's fashion collection, which I was strongly expecting, I decided with the approval of my husband and children that I would turn my total interest to the home collection with the same energy I used to put in the fashion collection, with

Printed, woven and knitted textiles patterned in strong shapes and stripes constitute an instantly recognizable look from Missoni Home.

a difference: the fashion collection had become for me more a duty than a passion while I could feel I had enough passion for the home to rejuvenate the home collection with a stronger design focus.'

Initially a modest range of bedding and towels, produced and distributed by T&J Vestor, a company founded by her grandparents in 1920, the current collection of bath and bedlinen, upholstery fabrics, curtains, rugs, lamps, pillows and throws now represents 20% of the Missoni wholesale turnover. Rosita Missoni is a regular collector of vintage pieces. One of her finds is a 1960s Verner Panton rocking chair, which she reupholstered in one of her fabrics, subsequently convincing the Panton estate to start manufacturing the chair once again, and using Missoni fabrics. The Missoni aesthetic is rapidly progressing from personal to public space with the expansion of the label into a chain of hotels. 'Transferring sensations from small rooms to large spaces isn't easy....For me, luxury is having time, being able to spoil other people, to dream a little....Spaces that are big, but liveable, large but intimate – a subtle and sophisticated aesthetic that shuns the obvious and the excessive.' Milan-based architect Matteo Thun, designer of the Missoni store in Manhattan, will be responsible for the design and planning of the thirty hotels expected to be open or under development by the year 2010.

The hotel as destination

Anonymous corporate hotels that provide only the utilities and are convenient, dependable and functional are far removed from the experience of the couture hotel, where the hotel itself is the destination. Visiting a couture hotel allows for the possibility of experiencing the designer's aesthetic without the commitment of buying into the look permanently.

Versace was the first fashion house to extend its brand identity into the couture hotel and hospitality market with the opening of Palazzo Versace on Australia's Gold Coast in 2000 and a second one in Dubai. Giancarlo Di Risio, the chief executive of this, the ultimate Italian luxury lifestyle brand, decided to focus on the high end of the luxury business, rather than expanding into cheaper goods for the mass market. This has resulted in what Donatella Versace, the creative director of the company, refers to as 'a 360-degree lifestyle, 365 days a year'.[1] Hotel interiors

'A 360-degree lifestyle, 365 days a year.'

Donatella Versace

Italian fashion designer Gianni Versace's former mansion, Casa Casuarinas in Florida's Miami beach resort, has been transformed into a hotel that has all the hallmarks of Versace couture: lavish embellishment, rich surfaces and opulent detailing.

are an ideal showcase for the various wares of a brand: furniture, bedlinen, porcelain and glassware, even designer chocolate. Brand-conscious consumers are not only able to 'live the dream', they can take it home with them too, as all the homewares and furnishings are for sale.

Other labels that are capitalizing on the consumers' desire for a total lifestyle experience include the Italian jewelry company's Bulgari Resort in Bali, and Alberta Ferretti's Carducci Hotel in Cattolica on the Atlantic Riviera in Italy. Most designers, however, content themselves with styling a series of rooms and suites, rather than operating as hoteliers. Vera Wang's suite for the Halekulani Hotel in Honolulu and Christian Lacroix's design for the Hotel Du Petit Moulin in Paris both offer an experience of the designers' complete vision, and the Chanel suite at the Paris Ritz even features double-C printed bathmats. Bottega Veneta has rooms in the St Regis hotel on New York's Fifth Avenue

designed by its creative director Tomas Maier in the Bottega Veneta signature style, with bark leather 'intrecciatto' weave trash bins and letter boxes, providing a showcase for the company's expansion into the furniture market.

The couture hotel is a contemporary phenomenon, a logical extension of lifestyle marketing and an irresistible opportunity for the brand to extend their remit into an ever wider market without compromising the quality of the product. Hotels have always been designed by the foremost interior practitioners of the day, such as interior decoration legend Dorothy Draper's 1940s extravaganza for Rio de Janeiro's Quitandinha. The difference now lies in the fact that it is the fashion designers who have taken over as the purveyors of luxury. It is *their* names that sell a product and represent a particular commitment to style and luxury, rather than that of an anonymous decorator or the reputation of the standards and service of the hotel itself.

The Versace label's trademark of the head of Medusa, a Chthonic female character who turned onlookers to stone, was adopted by Gianni Versace as his crest. It symbolizes the shocking and dangerous allure of the label's decadence and high glamour.

French fashion couturier Christian Lacroix collaborated with owner Nadia Murano to transform this seventeenth-century house in the Marais district in Paris into the Hotel Du Petit Moulin. The interior, described by Lacroix as a 'mixture of fashion and theatre', is an eclectic mix of antique and mid-century-modern furniture. The dramatic colours and multipatterned, embellished surfaces are also to be seen in his catwalk collections (above).

'Real luxury,' as defined by Armani, 'should be based on values such as craftsmanship, unique materials, timelessness and quality. I think it's a combination of comfort and sophistication, functionality and elegance.'[2] Undeniably welcome attributes, but the appeal of the couture hotel also lies in consumer recognition of not only the brand, but also its associations with social aspirations and like-minded fellow travellers.

The first of many Armani hotels will open in Milan in 2008 with plans to have an Armani hotel in every important city in the world over the next ten years. Each hotel will be fully furnished with Armani/Casa bespoke home collections and there will be 'luxury residences' adjacent to each hotel that will benefit from the hotel's services. The danger for any brand that hopes to be represented in every major city lies in the sheer scale of the enterprise, with the result that the couture hotel may become just one of many chains that service the global

hospitality market. The minimalist design hotel has already had its moment in time, acknowledged even by its progenitor, Ian Schrager, to be an outdated concept with its futuristic fittings and sleek contours. 'It's over for design hotels,' he claims. 'What was once the exception is now the rule. It doesn't interest me any more. I'm trying to change the game again.'[3]

To be convincing the couture hotel must be idiosyncratic, necessarily luxurious, eclectic in its interior and, most importantly of all, have a unique point of view. As American designer David Rockwell points out, 'Whether it's a residential building we're designing or a hotel or a restaurant, I think that the most important thing is to come up with a unique DNA, so that it has an authenticity to it and is not just a composite of various things we've seen and liked. I do think that people are very sensitive to authenticity.'[4]

The couture hotel at its best offers visitors and guests a theatrical experience

The hotel as home. The relaxed country-house style of Charlton House appeals in part because of its rural location in Somerset, with commensurate activities on offer – riding, walking, golf and archery – that allow the visitor a glimpse of a more measured and traditional way of English country life.

in which they become characters in the narrative – the nature of the drama depending on their mood or their aspirations. Reviews of these hotels use the language of the theatre critic: 'a dramatic and daring reinvention of the urban resort', 'smart, witty and sophisticated', 'a destination suspended in time and space'. A couture hotel may offer innovative design to the avant-garde, reference the 1980s with its uber-glam maximalism or even evoke nostalgia by creating the ambience of a private house and a vanishing aspect of English country living.

Location is also important in reinforcing the designer's vision: from contemporary urban environments that resonate with cutting-edge culture to the South Beach style of Casa Casuarina in Florida's Miami, once the home of Gianni Versace and decorated with all the glamorous excess you would expect of the fashion label. Conversely, the classic English look – trenchcoat, cashmere twinset and tweed skirt – is brought to mind by the rural environs of

the English countryside, the site of Charlton House, on the edge of the Somerset levels. Owned by Roger Saul, founder in 1971 of Mulberry, the British fashion, interiors and accessories label, the house is furnished in the label's signature style of traditional materials such as tweeds and checks. The seventeenth-century stone-built manor house with mullioned windows and furnished with antiques is representative of the quintessential country house style, a look popularized by decorator John Fowler. Together with his partner at Colefax and Fowler, Nancy Lancaster, he created a classic English style that set the fashion for interiors in the two decades following World War II, a look that also influenced international style, including American designer Ralph Lauren.

The experience of the g hotel in Galway, Ireland, is one of Hollywood glamour mediated through 1950s elegance, epitomized by the *Vogue* cover shot of model Jean Patchett by Irving Penn displayed in the hot pink lounge. Couture milliner

and native of Galway Philip Treacy has designed the interiors with the attention to detail and scrupulous regard for scale, colour and proportion that he gives to his couture hats. From the shocking pink colour of the walls and the dazzling op art carpet to the fragile winged chair backs, the hotel's ambience is animated by some of the atmosphere of the couturier's salon. Fashion drawings by leading illustrator David Downton, featuring catwalk models such as Linda Evangelista and Erin O'Connor, all wearing Philip Treacy hats, add to the experience. Four hundred silver mirror ball lights by designer Tom Dixon illuminate the grand salon and a flock of origami cranes by artist Eva Menz are suspended over the stairwell of the spa. 'Walking into the hotel will be a "movie star" experience,' Treacy confirmed before the opening of the hotel in 2005. 'It will be like walking into a film set. Guests will experience the hotel in quite individual ways, depending on their own response to it. It will be eclectic, and it

Couture milliner Philip Treacy returned to his Irish home town of Galway to undertake the creative direction of the g hotel, in collaboration with local architects Douglas Wallace.

There are an increasing number of female
executives visiting hotels for either business
purposes or to enjoy being pampered as an
antidote to the pressures of contemporary life.
The hotel is no longer a male bastion, it has
become increasingly feminized, and the spa is
now an essential element of the hotel experience.

Casa Camper is one of the few hotels to address the issues of recycling and sustainability. This ethos is reflected in the simplicity of the interiors – soft furnishings are at a minimum (helpful for the allergic and requiring less ecologically unsound laundering) – and the use of bicycles to tour the neighbourhood is encouraged.

Overleaf. The uncluttered interior of Casa Camper. Facing a courtyard, the bathroom looks out over a vertical garden of steel shelving and plants erected by the architect.

will seek to surprise. It will be all this and more but, above all, it will be glamorous.'

Where the g hotel hinges on its association with glamour and celebrity, Casa Camper is more an extension of an ethic, rather than an aesthetic. It is not a licensed brand extension, but an hotel entirely in keeping with the projected philosophy of the Spanish shoe company; providing a fusion between traditional craftsmanship and the avant-garde and placed in the urban, multicultural environs of Barcelona. The unassuming façade simply illuminated with the neon HOTEL sign fronts an interior that is both informal and unexpected, from the vertical garden to the hammocks. The informality extends to the bicycles hung from the ceiling for the use of guests, a decision that reflects the hotel's awareness of the need to be ecologically sound. Furthermore, the water heating system uses solar energy and the water supply undergoes chemical-free recycling. The Camper hotel can be seen as being at

the forefront of an ever increasing trend for responsible consumerism, as noted by Matteo Thun, architect and designer. 'Since 11 September there has been a design revolution. The collapse of the economy has caused the collapse of unnecessary consumerism. Sustainability will replace it.'[5]

This seems unlikely; it is clear from advance publicity that there is to be a substantial increase in the visibility of the couture hotel in most major cities and holiday venues. Luxury brands are intent on offering the 360-degree lifestyle dream to an ever increasing market. As global fashion companies such as Versace and Armani have to strictly control their brand identity through the homogenization of design, and as similar luxury brands and services become increasingly accessible, there will need to be in place a further differential to retain aspects of exclusivity. It is almost inevitable that this exclusivity will lie in the hotel as private home or club, rigorously anti-brand; and not about the product, but the experience.

La Maison Unique Longchamp, the French luggage and accessories label's New York store, is the work of London-based designer Thomas Heatherwick, who also designed for the company the leather and canvas expandable bag constructed from zip fasteners. The store is representative of the need for extraordinary space in selling a brand successfully in an increasingly competitive marketplace.

Smoke and mirrors

Fashion designers increasingly realize the importance of providing remarkable retail space, resulting in collaborations with architects and designers that serve to further their vision and reflect the aesthetic of the label. Frank Gehry's New York store for Issey Miyake and the work of Philippe Starck for Jean Paul Gaultier in Paris are both examples of the desire of the label to project its unique qualities and prestige. As Professor Christopher Breward, deputy head of research at the Victoria & Albert Museum, writes, 'The shop in its broadest definition is the last significant staging post in the trail of the product from design and manufacture to the intimate realm of the wearer, and as such strategies by which its goods are presented for sale are of prime importance in establishing a sense of what fashion is at any given time or place.'[7] Retail space is what convinces the buyer to buy, and the customer has grown indifferent to the bland, alienating spaces of minimalism.

When Longchamp, the French luxury accessories brand, commissioned British designer Thomas Heatherwick to design La Maison Unique Longchamp, the newest expansion for the brand in the USA in New York's Soho, his prime concern was to entice the customer over the threshold. Longchamp's one-hundredth boutique worldwide, as well as its new professional trade showroom, is housed on a surface area of more than 9,000 square feet (836 square metres). A monumental stairway made of steel ribbon strips connects the first floor to the primary retail space and provides a stunning entrance. Heatherwick explains, 'I wanted to make a big gesture. It needed not to feel like a staircase, a staircase is hard work. I wanted to make a landscape, more like a hillside that you wend your way up. It's important that there wasn't an element of anti-climax.' The staircase weighs 55 tonnes and took over six months to construct, leading to a wood-panelled

'The fashion commodity depends for its effectiveness on the expensive support of all the smoke and mirrors that the retailers can muster in their bid for a successful sale.'

Christopher Breward[6]

The Georgian home of fashion classicist Jasper Conran's flagship London store at 36 Sackville Street, Mayfair, is an exquisite realization of the couturier's salon, selling all aspects of Conran's high-end collections and offering a bespoke furniture line.

shop floor that displays the company's entire range for men and women.

Trained in three-dimensional design at London's Royal College of Art, where he is now senior fellow, Heatherwick has a multidisciplinary design practice that includes both sculpture and architecture. He is renowned for such diverse activities as the retractable rolling bridge and the 'Bleigiessen' installation for the Wellcome Trust in London. His application of 'strategic thinking' to designing a leather and canvas expandable bag with a spiral zipper for the accessories brand resulted in the commission from Longchamp's owners, the Cassegrain family, to design the store. Jean Cassegrain explains, 'the bag was a great concept, simple but original, we wanted to create the same excitement in the store; we wanted a sculpture rather than a stairway.' At the leading edge of modern design, Heatherwick values innovation. 'It is important to move life forward; I want to feel that we are in environments

that challenge us, that throw me off my normal assumptions and presumptions. It is a very exciting place to be in.'[8]

Certain shops enter the mythology of retail history, and make their mark with a single point of view through their singular understanding of the avant-garde, not only in fashion, but also in art, design, literature and music. The Parisian boutique Colette, sited on the rue Saint-Honoré, and opened in March 1997, was one of the first lifestyle shops to sell fashion and interior products alongside each other. Colette's ability to seize on the most radical and significant items from the catwalk or the counter-culture, together with an array of merchandise from around the globe, has made this eclectic lifestyle boutique one of the most influential stores in Europe. The boutique's basement houses a 'water-bar' selling ninety different types of water in a minimalist space designed by Arnaud Montigny and furnished by Belgian designer Maarten Van Severen.

Pioneering boutique Colette on Paris's rue St-Honoré is an aesthetic and cultural showground of all that is fashionable in clothes, art and music. Tapping into the trend for the esoteric, the water bar in the basement, designed by Arnaud Montigny and furnished by Belgium designer Maarten Van Severen, sells ninety different types of water, including one composed of 7,800 drops of Tasmanian rainwater.

This spread and overleaf. The starting point for London-based designer Allegra Hicks is always her textile designs for printed and woven fabrics, which feed into her fashion and interior ranges. These become the genesis of the luxury lifestyle brand that transmutes her version of bohemian glamour into interiors and onto the catwalk.

The antithesis of the grand gesture of the architect-designed store or the singular boutique are those emporia that reflect the qualities that we look for in a home. Ralph Lauren was one of the first brands to position his fashion in furnished rooms that reflected the aesthetic of the label. International luxury lifestyle brand Allegra Hicks is another. The designer engages with all aspects of design, being one of the few designers to start her practice in interiors and move successfully into fashion, rather than the more usual route of establishing a fashion label followed by designing for interiors. Hicks was already established as a designer for interior textiles before embarking on a fashion range, fuelled by her success in reinventing the kaftan in 1998, now a summer staple. The flagship store on London's Pont Street, just off Sloane Street, designed by her husband Ashley Hicks, showcases the ready-to-wear fashion and beach collection, homeware and interior textiles in room settings; with a drawing

room, library, dining room and bedroom all furnished in the label's products.

Allegra Hicks studied design at the Politecnico in Milan, before going on to study fine art in Brussels, a background that informs the designer's aesthetic of calm, sophisticated colours and simple graphic patterning, equally appealing whether on a rug, bed linen or a dress. The look is coherent and subtle, the simplicity of the designs upheld by the limited number of colours used in each design, never more than four or five screens. 'One design can be used in so many different ways. I love to change scale and colour and make motifs travel through print, embroidery and weave.' The rugs are distributed through The Rug Company and the wallpapers through the Paint & Paper Library.

The homogeneous branding inherent in the big labels is also an anathema to British designer Paul Smith. He has always offered a diverse range of products outside his fashion range that reflect his approach to

The antithesis of the lifestyle store, Paul Smith's London Mayfair shop exhibits a plethora of unexpected products in artless, abandoned display. The juxtaposition of diverse objects, all collected and sourced by Smith, is far removed from the over-styled formality of most retail outlets.

merchandising. Now with a turnover of £250 million, the latest addition to his retailing empire is located in London's Mayfair on Albemarle Street and is an emporium of personally chosen furniture, lights, paintings, toys and books that betray his singular preoccupations. An inveterate collector on his many travels of the idiosyncratic, the unusual and the overlooked, it takes the curatorial eye of Smith to retrieve such diverse items as antique rice chests from Japan and 1950s copies of *Domus* magazine. 'Initially the shop was selling items from my huge collections, but as we have sold so much we are now busy finding interesting items from around the world and so my role is that of curator rather than buyer.'

Specially chosen pieces of furniture, from a Louis XIV chair to a piece of mid-century modern, are reupholstered or decorated in unexpected fabrics and colours. The designer explains, 'we translate a lot of our prints from clothes into hard-wearing fabrics, which we use to customize

our antique furniture.' In selling *objets* rather than manufactured mass-produced products, he started the shop with no real expectation of commercial success, but saw it as a fantastically self-indulgent experiment. However, 'it has been incredibly successful from the beginning and really seems to show that people are looking for unusual pieces to have in their homes.'

Designer Orla Kiely concurs. 'People love their homes now more than ever, and are being much more creative in furnishing them. They are always searching for special things.' The designer's sophisticated grasp of the contextualization of pattern with products has resulted in a range of furniture to add to the already successful accessories line, interior and homeware products and men and women's fashion ranges. 'I've always loved the designs of the 1950s and 1960s. Danish design is a huge influence, I love hunting in flea markets and finding pieces.' Together with fellow designer Gerry Taylor, Kiely has worked

on developing a small range of furniture
to retail in the flagship store on London's
Monmouth Street, where the diversity of
the designer's aesthetic is evident. From
the fashion and furniture on display to
the custom-made wallpaper and rugs,
each design discipline informs the other
in a coherence of pattern and style.

The trend for shops that reflect the
ambience of 'home' is a reflection of the
importance placed on the personal in a
twenty-first century fraught with insecurities
and real and imagined dangers. Very few
people can resist the urge to surround
themselves with the things that they love,
that reflect their preoccupations, taste
and character, rather than clothes and
interiors that conform to the rigours of
an impersonal design precept. Design has
moved on from, 'How does this product
function?' to 'How does this product
feel?'[9] Consumers now expect to have an
emotional response to their purchases, and
introduce them into an environment that
already contains old and favoured pieces
from the past, mementos and memorabilia
from travels and experience. These all go
into the surroundings that we call 'home'.

A cohesive vision, the London flagship
store of designer Orla Kiely brings together
all aspects of her practice. Her designs
seamlessly adapt to a variety of applications,
from bags to wallpaper to fashion.

Notes

Introduction

1 Dior, Christian. *Dior by Dior.* Weidenfeld & Nicolson 1957. Penguin Books Ltd (Paperback) 1958, p. 189.

2 Adolf Loos 1899 essay, *'Das Prinzip der Bekleidung'* has been translated as 'The Principle of Cladding' by Jane Newman and John Smith in *Spoken into the Void; Collected essays 1897-1900.* MIT Press 1987, pp. 66–9. Quoted in Quinn, Bradley. *The Fashion of Architecture.* Berg 2003, p. 103.

3 Sudjic, Deyan. 'Building a Bolder Future.' *The Observer, Review.* 20 August 2006, p. 8.

4 Hudson, Jennifer. *1,000 New Designs and Where to Find Them. A 21st Century Source Book.* Laurence King Publishing 2006.

5 *Elle Decoration* June 2006, p. 86.

6 Woolman Chase, Edna and Ilka Chase. *Always in Vogue.* Victor Gollancz Ltd 1954.

7 Dixon, Tom. 'I'm Aiming for Global Domination.' Talib Choudhry. *The Sunday Times, Style Magazine* 27 August 2006, pp. 54, 55.

8 York, Peter. 'From Victorian Values to a Licence to Print Money.' *The Sunday Times* 23 July 2006, p. 3.

Chapter one: Inspiration

1 'The Secret World of Haute Couture.' BBC4 directed by Maggie Kinmouth, 6 November 2006.

2 Anna Wintour. American *Vogue.* November 2006.

3 Scott, Grant and Samantha Scott-Jeffries. *At Home with the Makers of Style.* Thames & Hudson 2005, p. 233.

4 Tungate, Mark. *The Times, T2* 21 July 2005.

5 Cliff, Stafford. *Home. What our Homes Really Mean to Us.* Quadrille 2006, p. 14.

6 Trendstop.com

7 De Botton, Alain. *The Architecture of Happiness.* Hamish Hamilton 2006, p. 68.

8 Guild, Tricia. *Cool Colours for Modern Living.* Quadrille 1999, p. 8.

Chapter two:
The Fashionability of Taste

1 Scott, Grant and Samantha Scott-Jeffries. *At Home with the Makers of Style.* Thames & Hudson 2005, p. 229.

2 Bayley, Stephen. *Taste. The Secret Meaning of Things.* Faber & Faber 1991, p. 12.

3 Breward, Christopher. *Fashion.* Oxford University Press 2003 p. 169.

4 Ibid note 1., p. 136.

5 Adapted from Gustav Pazaurek, catalogue of the Museum of Art Indiscretions, 1909.

6 Bayley, Stephen. 'Chair Wars'. *The Observer, Magazine* 10 September 2006, p. 31.

7 Loos (1900) 'Ladies Fashion', in Loos (1982), p. 99; see also Wollen (1987) and Loos (1964). See Wilson, Elizabeth. 'The Sphinx in the City. Urban Life, the Control of Disorder and Women.' University of California Press Ltd, Oxford, England 1991, p. 91.

8 Cliff, Stafford. *Home. What our Homes Really Mean to Us.* Quadrille 2006, p. 11.

9 Birtwell, Celia. 'Personal Space'. *Observer, Woman,* No. 8 August 2006, p. 43.

10 Bemelmans, Ludwig. *To the One I Love the Best. Episodes from the life of Lady Mendl.* Hamish Hamilton 1955, pp. 17, 25.

11 Ibid., p. 84.

12 Cliff, Stafford. *Home. What our Homes Really Mean to Us.* Quadrille 2006, p. 62.

13 Bayley, Stephen. *Taste. The Secret Meaning of Things.* Faber & Faber 1991, p. 140.

14 Cliff, Stafford. *Home. What our Homes Really Mean to Us.* Quadrille 2006, p. 62.

15 'The Best of Interiors.' *World of Interiors.* 'Private Chatsworth.' First published October 2001.

Chapter three: Threads

1 Evans, Caroline. *Fashion at the Edge. Spectacle, Modernity and Deathliness.* Yale University Press 2003, p. 261.

2 Lehl, Jürgen. *Koromo, Jürgen Lehl's Fabrics, Photographed by Yuriko Takagi.* Kenichi Kamai/Treville Co. Ltd 1999, p. 7.

3 Shah, David. 'Milior: a New Set of Rules' *Textile View* 2006, pp. 228–9.

4 Ansome, Carolyn. *The Times* 19 September 2006, p. 27.

5 http://www.designboom.com/eng/interview/wanders.html

Chapter four: Liaisons

1 Roux, Caroline. 'A Milan for all Seasons'. *The Observer, Magazine* 23 April 2006, p. 60.

2 Appleyard, Bryan. 'Want Taste Today? Get Bags of Money'. *The Sunday Times* 29 January 2006, p. 8.

3 'People Now. Vivienne Westwood'. *Elle Decoration* September 2005, p. 57.

4 'International Textiles Interior'. *Spanish Fashion Underfoot* August/September 2006, p. 42.

5 Armstrong, Lisa. 'Is That a Sofa on the Catwalk?' *The Times* 21 June 2006.

6 Issey Miyake, 'The Dream Weaver.' Business Week Online – MSNBC.com Reena Jana.

7 Thompson, Henrietta. 'Cross Dressing.' *Blueprint Architecture, Design, Culture* May 2006, No. 242, pp. 71–6.

Chapter five: House Style

1 Long, Carola. *The Times, Bricks and Mortar* 22 September 2006, p. 18.

2 Ibid.

3 Bowes, Gemma. 'The Death of the Design Hotel.' *The Observer, Escape* 18 June 2006.

4 Cliff, Stafford. *Home. What our Homes Really Mean to Us.* Quadrille 2006, p. 124.

5 Bowes, Gemma. 'The Death of the Design Hotel.' Escape. *The Observer* 18 June 2006.

6 Breward, Christopher. *Fashion.* Oxford University Press 2003, ch. 7 'Shopping for Style', p. 156.

7 Ibid., p. 143.

8 'Imagine.' Alan Yentob profile of Thomas Heatherwick BBC1. 6 June 2006.

9 Kjaer, Anne. 'Lifestyle.' *Textile View* magazine 2006, p. 30.

Bibliography

Bayley, Stephen. *Taste. The Secret Meaning of Things.* Faber & Faber. 1991.

Belanger Grafton, Carol. *Victorian Goods and Merchandise, 2,300 Illustrations.* Dover Publications Inc. 1997.

Bemelmans, Ludwig. *To the One I Love the Best. Episodes from the Life of Lady Mendl (Elsie de Wolfe).* Hamish Hamilton. 1955.

Black, Sandy. *Fashioning Fabrics. Contemporary Textiles in Fashion.* Black Dog Publishing Ltd. 2006.

Black, Sandy. *Knitwear in Fashion.* Thames & Hudson. 2002.

Braddock, Sarah E. and Marie O'Mahony. *Techno Textiles. Revolutionary Fabrics for Fashion and Design.* Thames & Hudson. 1998.

Breward, Christopher. *Fashion.* Oxford University Press. 2003.

Cliff, Stafford. *Home. What our Homes Really Mean to Us.* Quadrille. 2006.

Cohen, Deborah. *Household Gods.* Yale University Press. 2006.

Conniff, Richard. *The Natural History of the Rich. A Field Guide.* William Heinemann. 2003.

De Botton, Alain. *The Architecture of Happiness.* Hamish Hamilton. 2006.

Guild, Tricia. *Cool Colours for Modern Living.* Quadrille Publishing Ltd. 1999.

Jackson, Lesley. *Twentieth-Century Pattern Design: Textile and Wallpaper Pioneers.* Mitchell Beazley. 2002.

Lehl, Jürgen. *Koromo, Kenichi Kawai. Jürgen Lehl's Fabrics, photographed by Yuriko Takagi.* Treville Co. Ltd. 1999.

Quinn, Bradley. *The Fashion of Architecture.* Berg. 2003.

Scott, Grant and Samantha Scott-Jeffries. *At Home with the Makers of Style.* Thames & Hudson. 2005.

Sparke, Penny. *As Long as it's Pink. The Sexual Politics of Taste.* Pandora/HarperCollins. 1995.

Woolman Chase, Edna and Ilka Chase. *Always in Vogue.* Victor Gollancz Ltd. 1954.

Yokoo, Tadanori. *Made in Japan. The Textiles of Jürgen Lehl.* Parco View. 1983.

Acknowledgments

Thanks to Helen Evans at Laurence King
Publishing, Eleanor Ridsdale of Rudd Studio, and
most particularly to Catherine Hooper of Hoop
Design and photographer Allan Hutchings; Adam
Walker at Zaha Hadid, Alexis Nishihata at Bill
Amberg, Alice Panzer at Vitra, Alison Smith at Paul
Smith, Allegra Hicks, Amanda Warren at Rosenthal,
Ana Abramcyk of Edun, Andrew Stanislaw at
Wedgwood, Angel Monzon of Vessel, Bella Clark
at Celia Birtwell, Bill Amberg, Carey Young, Celia
Birtwell, Christina Yu at Neisha Crosland, Christine
Mulvad at Day Birger et Mikkelsen, Christopher
and Suzanne Sharp of The Rug Company, DAC,
David Mills at Jasper Conran, Deborah Milner, Earl
Singh, Edun, Ellen Pinto at Pantone, Eva Takamine
at Jürgen Lehl, Giovanna Golnelli at Fendi, Gisela
Torres, Glenys Hollingsworth, Hannah Phipps at
Attenborough/Saffron, Hannah Woodward at
Interdesign, Heti Gervis at Hargreaves-Gervis,
Jaime Hayon, Jasper Conran, Jo Walton, John
Angus, Julius Walters of Stephen Walters and Son,
Jürgen Lehl, Karen Nicol, Kate Box at Orla Kiely,
Kirsty Philip at Habitat, Laura Partridge at Orla
Kiely, Linlee Allen at Colette, Louise Davinson
at Day Birger et Mikkelsen, Louise Hindley at
Charlton House, Marianne Brandi of Day Birger
et Mikkelsen, Marilyn Rowe at Wedgwood,
Marina Eleonor Robles at Ailanto, Mark Eley and
Wakako Kishimoto of Eley Kishimoto, Nancy
at Issey Miyake, Nelly Rodi, Neisha Crosland,
Nicole Farhi, Nina Farnell-Watson at Philip
Treacy, Piers Smerin & Nick Eldridge of Eldridge
Smerin, Orla Kiely, Patricia Belford, Dr Philippa
Woodcock, Rachel Linford at Orla Kiely, Robert
Alcalay at Allegra Hicks, Ron Aram, Rosie Farrer
at SCP, Sir Paul Smith, Ruth Coughlan at Camper,
Sarah Nelson at Etro, Selim Bayer, Sheridan
Coakley of SCP, Tena Strok at Kastini, Dr Tim
Willey, Tony Davis of Art Meets Matter, Yuka
Taniguchi of the NUNO Corporation, and to my
dearest daughter Emily, and to stalwart friends
Pam Hemmings and Jenny and Peter Hoon.

Picture credits

Ailanto: 144, 145, 162, 163

Allan Hutchings Photography: 26 left and 3rd from left, 30 bottom left, 31 right, 42, 43, 44, 48, 49, 50, 51, 52, 53, 61, 64 bottom left and 3rd from left, 73, 74, 75, 76, 77, 78, 118, 119, 120, 121, 122, 123 left, 173 right, 198, 199, 200, 201, 215

Bill Amberg: 45

Basso & Brooke: 143 left, 168, 169

Bill Batten, House & Garden copyright. The Conde Nast Publications Ltd.: 109

Selim Bayer (Eldridge-Smerin): 136, 137

John Angus: 34

Armani Casa: 83

B&B Italia: 65 centre, 70–71

Bettmann/Corbis: 147

Christophe Bielsa (www.paris-hotel-petitmoulin.com): 177 bottom right, 190, 191 right

Hélène Binet: 11

C Osterreichische Galerie Belvedere, Vienna, Austria, The Bridgeman Art Library: 30 right, 69

Jean François Carley (Edun): 126 right, 127

Charlton House: 176 left, 192, 193

Colette: 206, 207

Jasper Conran: 27 left and far right, 40, 41, 152 left, 153, 155, 204, 205

Corbis: 186

Neisha Crosland: 86–87

Day Birger et Mikkelsen: 18, 19, 27 centre, 33

Dover Publications Inc: 68

Sally Edwards: 124, 125

Eley Kishimoto: 104, 105, 148, 149

Eric Robert/Corbis Sygma: 142 bottom, 146

Etro: 16, 17, 100, 101, 102, 103

Beth Evans (Celia Birtwell): 2, 88, 89, 90, 91

Nicole Farhi: 180

Fendi: 175, 178, 179

Fernando & Humberto Campana: 98 top left, 135

Marnie Fogg: 13, 93

Grazia magazine: 12

Habitat: 164, 165, 166

Hans Hansen/Marc Eggimann copyright Vitra, chair by Verner Panton: 65 left

Hargreaves-Gervis: 54, 56, 57

Stuart Haygarth: 139

Jaime Hayon: 32, 65 right, 79, 176 2nd from left

Heimtextil: 38, 39

Allegra Hicks: 208, 209, 210–11

Marc Jacobs 154

Justin de Villeneuve Getty Images: 167

Yoshiharu Koizumi (Jürgen Lehl): 98 bottom centre, 99 centre, 115, 116, 141

Rachel Linford (Orla Kiely): 59, 60

Longchamp: 202, 203

Sue McNab (NUNO): 112, 113

Missoni Home: 6 left, 7 centre, 8, 9, 15, 176 4th and 5th from left, 182, 183, 184,185

Issey Miyake: 170,171

Monogram Hotels: 177 left and right, 194, 196, 197

Chris Moore: 14, 28, 30 top left, 31 left, 80 right, 82, 84, 99 left, 123 right, 126 left, 132, 133, 150, 157 left, 161 right, 181, 188 right, 191 left, 212 right

Noboru Morikawa (Jürgen Lehl): 114

Karen Nicol: 46, 47, 98 bottom right, 106, 107

Patrick Norguet: 151

Pantone: 58

Roche-Bobois: 134

Nelly Rodi: 35

Rosenthal: 176 3rd from left, 187, 189

Sainsbury's magazine: 138

Daniel Schweitzer: 67

SCP: 20, 21, 72

Simon Upton Archive Interiors: 97

Sir Paul Smith: 22, 23, 25, 172, 173 left, 212 left, 213

Paul Smith: 27 right, 63

Philippe Starck: 80

Eva Takamine (Jürgen Lehl) www.jurgenlehl.jp: 98 left, 117

Tino Tedaldi: 4, 64 right, 85

The Future Laboratory www.thefuturelaboratory.com: 36–37

The Rug Company: 142, left and centre, 143 centre and right, 156, 157 right, 158, 159, 160, 161 left

Gisela Torres (Whistles): 64 top left, 92, 94, 95

Philip Treacy: 195

Chris Tubbs, Red Cover Picture Resource: 81

Patricia Urquiola: 110

Manuel Vason: 98 top right, 128, 129, 130–31 (Clothes: Deborah Milner, Film direction: Peter Gray and Johnny Wilkinson, Hair: Peter Gray at Untitled, Make Up: Florrie White at Holy Cow, Models: Rima and Mateja Penava, Production: Alexander Tovey, Photography Assistants: Linda Brownlee and Toby Hudson, Assistants to Peter Gray: K Kay, Masa, Reiko and Sue, Assistants to Deborah Milner: Rogeria Porte, Phoebe O'Donnell, Karen Spurgin, Ela Pritchard, Sarah lee, Michelle Devine and Andre Roese, Location: The Wapping Project, Lighting: Sola lights from Brieze, Thanks to Jules Wright at the Wapping project, Emma at Holy Cow, Victoria at Storm Models)

Marcel Wanders: 99 right, 111

Wedgwood: 152 right

Werner Huthmacher Berlin: 10

To my friend Caroline Cox

LAURENCE KING

Published in 2007
by Laurence King Publishing Ltd
361–373 City Road
London EC1V 1LR
United Kingdom
Tel: +44 20 7841 6900
Fax: +44 20 7841 6910
e-mail: enquiries@laurenceking.co.uk
www.laurenceking.co.uk

A catalogue record for this book is
available from the British Library.

ISBN 13: 978-1-85669-535-0
ISBN 10: 1-85669-535-2

Printed in China

Designer: Eleanor Ridsdale, Rudd Studio Ltd
Commissioning Editor: Helen Evans
Project Editor: Catherine Hooper
Picture Research: Marnie Fogg